THE WAR OF THE CAMISARDS (1702–1704)

THE WAR OF THE CAMISARDS (1702–1704)

Huguenot Insurrection during the Reign of Louis XIV

STEPHEN M. DAVIS

Foreword by
MICHAEL A. G. HAYKIN

WIPF & STOCK · Eugene, Oregon

THE WAR OF THE CAMISARDS (1702–1704)
Huguenot Insurrection during the Reign of Louis XIV

Copyright © 2024 Stephen M. Davis. All rights reserved. Except for brief quotations in critical publications or reviews, no part of this book may be reproduced in any manner without prior written permission from the publisher. Write: Permissions, Wipf and Stock Publishers, 199 W. 8th Ave., Suite 3, Eugene, OR 97401.

Wipf & Stock
An Imprint of Wipf and Stock Publishers
199 W. 8th Ave., Suite 3
Eugene, OR 97401

www.wipfandstock.com

PAPERBACK ISBN: 979-8-3852-2902-4
HARDCOVER ISBN: 979-8-3852-2903-1
EBOOK ISBN: 979-8-3852-2904-8

10/23/24

Scripture quotations are from the ESV® Bible (The Holy Bible, English Standard Version®), copyright © 2001 by Crossway, a publishing ministry of Good News Publishers. Used by permission. All rights reserved.

In memory of the French martyrs of the Church of the Desert
who defended religious freedom against state tyranny

Oh, how happy would I be if I were among the number of those whom the Lord has reserved to announce his praises and die for his interests.

Fulcran Rey, martyr for the faith (1688)

He walked to his execution as if he were going to a feast.

Eyewitness of Claude Brousson's execution (1698)

Save me, O God! For the waters have come up to my neck.

Pierre Séguier (1702)

Ah Monsieur, might it please God that I have a soul as beautiful as theirs.

Gentilhomme De Vilas to Bâville (1702)

Contents

Foreword by Michael A. Haykin | ix

Preface | xi

Introduction | xv

CHAPTER 1   Competing War Stories | 1
CHAPTER 2   Reformation and Repression | 7
CHAPTER 3   War and Broken Treaties | 14
CHAPTER 4   Protestantism Outlawed | 22
CHAPTER 5   Preachers and Prophets | 31
CHAPTER 6   Return from Exile | 38
CHAPTER 7   The Sword of Vengeance | 44
CHAPTER 8   Massacres and Retaliation | 50
CHAPTER 9   The Devastation of the Cévennes | 57
CHAPTER 10   The Beginning of the End | 63
CHAPTER 11   Negotiations and Surrender | 68
CHAPTER 12   Postscript to War | 76
CHAPTER 13   Conclusion | 83

Chronology | 89

From the Same Author | 95

Bibliography | 97

Index | 103

Foreword

At the very time that Martin Luther was coming to the convictions that would characterize the Reformation—*sola fide* and *sola gratia* and *solus Christus*—there was also a circle of French evangelicals whose views were moving in the same direction. In time, the biblical perspectives and preaching of these men would flower into what we call the French Reformation and produce that remarkable body of believers known as the Huguenots. The story of the French Reformation, the Huguenot churches, and their Protestant descendants is one that is largely unknown to Anglophone Protestants, and that is a genuine shame.

Given the major role that English-speaking Protestants have played in the building of their respective cultures since the close of the medieval era and then in taking the gospel to the ends of the earth in the past two hundred years, they have wrongly assumed that theirs is the central story in the kingdom of God during the modern era. Reinforcing this hubris has been the plethora of books in the English language dealing with literally every aspect of the Christian faith. But the story of French Protestantism—a specialty of Stephen Davis—is equally thrilling: it is one of the great stories of church history, a story of reform and revival, remarkable leaders and horrifying reverses, of divine glory and tragedy.

In this particular volume, Davis focuses on the tragic story of the revolt of the Camisards, the final episode in the French Wars of Religion, that series of religious wars that had begun

Foreword

shortly before the death of John Calvin in 1564. The War of the Camisards was a direct result of the deeply misguided belief held by the seventeenth-century French monarchy and ruling classes that Protestantism needed to be eliminated from French soil for the nation to flourish. The Revocation of the Edict of Nantes in 1685, accompanied by the resultant emigration of a few hundred thousand Protestants (an economic disaster since so many of those who left belonged to the burgeoning middle class), the shattering of Huguenot churches and their presbyteries as well as the brutal execution of a number of pastors like Claude Brousson (1647–98), led to the revolt of the Camisards and the emergence of the so-called French Prophets.

Andrew Fuller (1754–1815), the important Baptist leader at the turn of the nineteenth century, once noted that "when Christians have resorted to the sword in order to resist persecution for the gospel's sake, as did . . . the French protestants, and some others, within the last six hundred years, the issue has commonly been, that they have perished by it."[1] Fuller's observation is a just one: the use of the sword to advance and/or defend the gospel is not sanctioned by Holy Scripture. A point with which Davis concurs in this illuminating volume.

However, as Davis concludes, the failure of the Camisards is not the final act of French Protestantism—for did not our Lord say, "I will build my church, and the gates of hell shall not prevail against it"? Protestant pastors like Antoine Court (1696–1760)—for whom a substantial English biography is yet to be written—were raised up to restore the French Calvinist churches. Furthermore, as Davis rightly insists, the history of the Camisard War is at its root about that most vital of human liberties, the freedom of religious conviction and worship.

Michael A. G. Azad Haykin, ThD, FRHistS
Professor of Church History and Biblical Spirituality
The Southern Baptist Theological Seminary

---

1. Fuller, *Complete Works*, 206.

Preface

The War of the Camisards was the last of France's wars of religion. Nobles and princes led the early Wars of Religion from 1562 to 1598 in a kingdom where Protestantism threatened the Catholic Church and the monarchy. Protestants fielded large armies and had stunning victories. Entire cities were won over to the Reformed faith, and one out of twelve of the kingdom's subjects was Reformed. The kings of France were constrained to grant stronghold cities to Huguenots, among them Montauban, Nîmes, and especially La Rochelle.[2] Those decades of war ended with the conversion to Catholicism of Henry of Navarre, who was crowned Henry IV and enacted the Edict of Nantes in 1598, granting Protestants limited religious freedom.

As wars go, the War of the Camisards pales in comparison with the Wars of Religion of the 1500s. There were no nobles to lead the peasant armies, its active phase hardly lasted two years, and the war was limited to the Cévennes region in southern France. For two years, the royal troops of Louis XIV battled outnumbered, ill-equipped peasants led by wool combers, shepherds, and farmers. The war mobilized several great marshals of France and ended with negotiations between a decorated marshal of France and a modest baker, Jean Cavalier. Interest in the war has ebbed and waned over the last three hundred years. Yet the war produced an

---

2. See Brachet, *Etymological Dictionary of the French Language* for suggestions on the origin of the term *Huguenot* (200).

Preface

outsized interest in the press of its time. Several books were written shortly after the war ended, and hundreds have been written since then. The conflict remains a critical part of French religious history.[3]

The War of the Camisards has been both embraced and rejected by French Protestants. The primary causes for rejection are prophetism, nourished by Old Testament prophecies that God would pour out his Spirit in a time of trouble (Joel 2:28–30), and the prophetic call to violent resistance. Both were departures from classic Reformed teaching and were considered controversial. The war also raised serious questions. Were the Camisards justified in taking up arms against the French king? Were they traitors in calling upon foreign powers for assistance? Were the Camisards heroes fighting against oppression for the freedom of conscience or dangerous fanatics who engaged in atrocities? Were the prophets and prophetesses who accompanied the Camisards animated by the Spirit of God or a demonic spirit, or were they victims of psychological trauma? The explanations of theologians, historians, and sociologists have changed throughout the centuries. There are Protestant perspectives and Catholic ones. There are contradictory eyewitnesses to the events that took place. Those who claimed the Spirit's inspiration for the violence were convinced that God had called them to avenge the years of oppression and persecution. Those who opposed them believed they were doing God's work stamping out heresy.

My understanding of biblical teaching does not allow for prophets or new revelation after the apostolic period and the completion of the New Testament. Others are free to disagree. I was not an eyewitness to the events, and the phenomena remain shrouded in mystery and unanswered questions.[4] The Camisards' adversaries were persuaded that prophets and prophetesses were

---

3. Joutard, *Camisards*, 9–10.

4. See Chabrol, "Diffusion et filiations" (151–52) for the influence of French prophetism on other movements in England and the United States, including the Shakers, Quakers, and Methodists.

Preface

demon-possessed, and there is evidence of attempts at exorcism.[5] A more modern interpretation understands these manifestations as a kind of hysteria, a mental illness brought about by trauma. Others believed the prophets and prophetesses were imposters who were taught how to fake their behavior. That might be true in some cases, but it is difficult to believe they faked something for which they suffered dearly. These were people of conviction, a conviction that led many to excesses and execution or years as galley slaves.[6]

My aim is to tell the story from the historical claims as I found them with their contradictions.[7] Other questions need to be considered in light of this history. Did the Camisards' actions hasten the religious freedom finally granted decades later? If the Camisards cannot be exonerated for committing acts of violence, might their actions be understood as horrible necessities in light of their suffering and the injustices they endured? The Camisards are not without reproach. They cannot be absolved of the numerous atrocities they committed in their wrath or be transformed into chivalrous heroes. When speaking of atrocities of which they are accused, their enemies did the same and worse, leading to retaliation and cycles of violence. Voltaire's words should be remembered: "They acted like ferocious beasts, but their women and little ones had been taken. They tore to pieces the hunters who tracked them."[8]

---

5. Bost, "'Prophètes des Cévennes,'" 413.
6. Bost, "'Prophètes des Cévennes,'" 414.
7. All translations are my own.
8. Ducasse, *Guerre des Camisards*, 99.

Introduction

Voltaire wrote, "It is dreadful that the Christian Church has always been torn apart by dissension and that blood has flowed throughout the centuries by hands bearing the God of peace."[9] The reign of Louis XIV epitomized this dictum. In the late 1600s and early 1700s, following the Revocation of the Edict of Nantes, Protestant Huguenots worshipped illegally in secret places in the Cévennes region of southern France. For seventeen years after the Revocation, a rebellion simmered among the Huguenots. Their insurrection was not simply against crushing taxes and misery. The uprising sprang from an oppressed people after their temples were demolished, their pastors exiled, Bible reading and family worship outlawed, their children kidnapped, their homes pillaged, their women imprisoned, and their men sentenced for life on the king's galleys. When their pastors were exiled and the remaining preachers executed, the prophets and prophetesses (*inspirés*)[10] appeared and the Camisards arose in revolt, courageous and vengeful men of action. Early victories emboldened them, yet in the end, they were no match for heavily armed royal forces. One by one, their leaders surrendered or were killed. Survivors were allowed to leave the kingdom for countries of refuge.

---

9. Voltaire, *Siècle de Louis XIV*, 405.

10. The term *inspirés* (inspired ones) was used to describe prophets and prophetesses purportedly animated by the Holy Spirit.

Introduction

The War of the Camisards began in 1702 and ended with the death of the Camisard leader Roland in 1704. According to the last Camisard, Abraham Mazel, the word *Camisard* refers either to the white shirt (*chemise* or *camisole*) they wore over their clothing to be recognized among themselves or comes from *camisade*, referring to night attacks.[11] After 1704, there were skirmishes and further resistance; several Camisard leaders were executed in 1705, and there were renewed attempts of insurrection until 1710. These were times of forced conversions, exile, and misery for Protestants in the twilight years of Louis XIV's reign, which ended with his death in 1715. All attempts to convert Protestants after the Revocation had failed miserably. With echoes of the biblical exodus and wilderness wanderings, this period became known as the Church of the Desert. To defend their homes and religious liberty, peasant warriors launched the War of the Camisards and heroically battled numerically superior royal forces to reclaim their lost religious rights.

The philosophers of the Enlightenment found contemptible the intolerance of both the Catholic Church and the Huguenots. The prophetism was qualified as "fanaticism, obscurantism, illuminism, and blind and murderous passion." Even Protestant opinion of the eighteenth century was severe toward the rustic, poorly dressed Camisards, their self-appointed prophets and prophetesses, and "this phenomenon that especially touched the poor, peasants and artisans, and the illiterate."[12] The enthusiasm for the Camisards decreased between the two World Wars and was revived in the 1960s with historical works, fiction, television shows, and films. They were coopted by various groups for diverse purposes (revolutionaries, Marxism, '68 protests) without regard for their religious convictions. Since then, André Ducasse has written *La guerre des Camisards* (1962), Philippe Joutard, *Les Camisards* (1976), Lillian Crété, *Les Camisards* (1992), and Marianne Carbonnier-Burkard, *La révolte des Camisards* (2012). These books have been largely used in writing the present account. They

11. Carbonnier-Burkard, *Révolte des Camisards*, 6.
12. Chabrol, "Diffusion et filiations," 146–47.

INTRODUCTION

differ in some details, mainly dates and spelling of proper names, but agree in substance. I have also benefited from consulting the *Mémoires* of Louis XIV, Jean Cavalier, Jacques Bonbonnoux, Bâville, Villars, and others.

The first chapter presents Catholic and Protestant perspectives about the war. Chapters 2 and 3 provide background to understand why the War of the Camisards took place almost two hundred years after the Reformation first troubled the kingdom of France. In chapter 4, the stage for resistance was set when Louis XIV outlawed the Protestant religion in 1685 and persecuted the religious minority. Chapter 5 recounts the rise of preachers, prophets, and prophetesses to fill the vacuum left by exiled Reformed pastors after the Revocation of the Edict of Nantes. Chapter 6 describes the return from exile of Claude Brousson and François Vivent, who were martyred before the war broke out. Chapters 7 to 9 depict the outbreak of the War of the Camisards, major figures, and the devastation of the Cévennes region. In chapter 10 the war winds down as the Camisards find themselves with fewer military successes and unable to sustain the conflict. Chapter 11 announces the arrival of Marshal de Villars, whose change in tactics leads to negotiations and the surrender of the Camisards' greatest leader, Jean Cavalier. The postscript to war in chapter 12 describes the slow rebuilding of Reformed churches with a return to classic Reformed teachings under Antoine Court. The conclusion briefly addresses the contribution of the War of the Camisards to advances in religious freedom and the state of religion in France today.

This book does not seek to present the War of the Camisards as a model of resistance to tyrannical governments. But I hope the book might bring better understanding toward those who engaged in the struggle for religious freedom, to try to understand their times, and to understand our own.

CHAPTER 1

Competing War Stories

In the first centuries of the Reformation in France, Protestants paid dearly for their devotion to the gospel. They were afflicted with unimaginable suffering. When we remember the sufferings of the victims of intolerance, many of whom had loved ones in dungeons or as prisoners on the king's galley ships, we better understand any acts of desperation, even those acts that shock our sensibilities today. Ultimately, the greater part of the blame is on the persecutors. The persecuted Protestant minority had unceasingly affirmed their loyalty to the French Crown as subjects and their duty to God as Christians. There was no attempt to overthrow the king or disrupt society. They believed the end of their persecution would come with the monarch's conversion. After this divine intervention, France would be protected from the wars of religion in Europe, and without violence, Catholics and Protestants would reconcile. "Protestants saw no contradiction between their affirmation of fidelity [to the Crown] and their actions."[1]

The Catholic Church and public opinion of the time would disagree with this assessment. In September 1703, Bishop Esprit Fléchier of Nîmes addressed the ecclesiastics of his diocese in a

---

1. Joutard, *Camisards*, 157–58.

The War of the Camisards (1702–1704)

pastoral letter to console them. He colorfully described the disorder in the region of the Cévennes that he attributed to the Camisards and lamented the persecution against the Catholic Church in the murder of its priests, the Lord's anointed who "were the first victims that the fanatics slaughtered."[2] In this view, the priests were victims of fanatics who considered the Catholic religion detestable. The Camisards, animated by demonic voices mistaken for the Spirit's inspiration, began the rebellion with the murder of an abbot who "from his youth had been devoted to gospel missions and whose death signaled a widespread revolt in the parishes."[3] All attempts to bring the Camisards to reasonable obedience through patience and charity, and by fatherly warnings, had been in vain. This murderous sect shed the blood of priests, burned others, and even slit their throats at the altars at the time of holy sacrifice. The Camisards were debauched scoundrels and raving prophets who sold out to foreign interests and mindlessly followed orders from a secret consistory. Voilà, an oft-repeated perspective of Catholic opponents of the Camisards. Yet even Catholic writers like Brueys were constrained to recognize the truth of the accusations of torture at the hand of Abbot du Chaila, killed by the Camisards in 1702 and whose death triggered the War of the Camisards.[4]

Most Protestants would decry such a characterization. True, the Camisards regarded the ecclesiastics as their enemies who repeatedly solicited the king to permit violent persecution against their bodies, conscience, and possessions. These priests were not considered witnesses to the gospel but the principal cause that forced the Camisards to take up arms. If their consciences had not been violated through coerced conversions, their children kidnapped, and their men and women imprisoned, there would have been no reason for the rebellion. Any fanaticism was the fruit of ignorance and the absence of their pastors who had been exiled after the Revocation of the Edict of Nantes. Any patience and charity were rare toward Protestants. Violence against them

2. Fléchier, *Œuvres complètes*, 125.
3. Fléchier, *Œuvres complètes*, 126.
4. Puaux, "Origines, causes et conséquences," 210.

rendered them violent, although many of the atrocities attributed to the Camisards are unfounded. Their actions were justified in the struggle for freedom of conscience. They practiced the law of the talion and took vengeance on their enemies. The Camisards were heroes, and their actions led to religious freedom decades later when the government realized the price to pay to stamp out rebellions. Voilà, a Protestant perspective not shared by all.

There have been able defenders of Louis XIV, the Catholic Church, the Revocation of the Edict of Nantes, and the repression of the insurrection. They considered the Camisards robbers, scoundrels, and murderers. From a Catholic perspective, David-Augustin Brueys' *Histoire de fanatisme de Nostre Temps* (*History of Fanaticism of Our Times*) was written in the 1700s shortly after the war. He addressed New Converts (*Nouveaux Convertis*)[5] concerning the fanatics among them "who had renounced their religion before men, had fallen into insanity, and committed horrible attacks."[6] Jean-Baptiste L'Ouvreleul, priest of Saint-Germain-de-Calberte, ministered at the funeral service of the Abbot du Chaila. His book, *Histoire du fanatisme renouvelé* (*History of the Revival of Fanaticism*), was edited several times and republished in 2001. Hubert Bost calls it "the best [book] coming from the Catholic camp to understand the events and their impact on public opinion."[7]

Alexandre de Lamothe wrote *Les Camisards* at the end of the nineteenth century and blamed other historians for distorting the facts. For him, the Revocation was "far from being a crime."[8] It rectified the harm done by the Edict of Nantes when the Reformed religion forced Henry IV to offer it as a dangerous concession. Reformed believers were intolerant and divided the nation. They opposed Henry IV's successor, Louis XIII, and were crushed three times by the royalists, yet retained "the incredible advantages guaranteed by the Edict of Nantes." During the reign of Louis XIV, who

---

5. *Nouveaux Convertis* were Protestants who converted to Catholicism after the harsh measures afflicted on them.

6. Brueys, *Histoire du fanatisme*, iv–vi.

7. Bost, Review of *Histoire du fanatisme*, 443.

8. Lamothe, *Camisards*, 7.

sought the kingdom's unity through gentle persuasion, the Huguenots continued their machinations as a "sect and political party" and conspired with France's enemies to undermine his authority.[9] After decades of opposition, gentleness and patience toward Protestants were exhausted. The king had no other recourse than the suppression of the uprising. The king and all of France believed the Revocation was necessary, and insurrections were fomented by refugees in Geneva and paid for by foreign gold. According to Lamothe's figures, sixty thousand out of one million Huguenots emigrated to Switzerland, Holland, and England. Their flight "rid France of more enemies than good citizens."[10] I leave history and my readers to judge the truth of Lamothe's charges.

The Œuvres complètes of Bishop Fléchier provide a fascinating window into a Catholic viewpoint of the Camisard rebellion in Fléchier's letters to the faithful, priests, nuns, and the archbishop of Paris for advice in dealing with the New Converts. He understood that the king had "ordered the New Converts of his kingdom to profess the faith and follow the practices of the Catholic Church" and wanted to know whether the king desired to "abandon them to their consciences or pressure them with the weight of his royal authority."[11] Fléchier also expressed in his letters to the Court that "preaching, reason, disputation, conferences, charity, and pastoral care" had not advanced conversions among the recalcitrant Huguenots and they needed firm and consistent pressure to "make a public profession of the Catholic religion."[12]

Accusations against Huguenots continued in the eighteenth and nineteenth centuries. They were attacked for calling upon foreign powers to assist them in overthrowing the monarchy. They were treated as traitors and conspirators. Indeed, there was contact with Reformed countries of refuge, but these contacts date back to the sixteenth century, well before the Revocation. After 1661 there was an uninterrupted flow of refugees to friendly nations.

9. Lamothe, *Camisards*, 8–9.
10. Lamothe, *Camisards*, 10.
11. Fléchier, *Œuvres complètes*, 258–59.
12. Lemoine, *Mémoires des évêques*, 200.

From these countries, projects originated to support Reformed believers. If Protestants sought outside help in their troubles, they did no less than French Catholics supported by Catholic nations and Rome. Despite the persecutions, Protestants manifested loyalty toward the king and, apart from their consciences, a readiness to submit their lives to his authority. From their resignation was born the expression *"patient comme un Huguenot"* (patient as a Huguenot).[13]

The centuries following the War of the Camisards have seen these two stories repeated with variations. Many accounts on both sides lack support for the legends and myths surrounding the Camisards or the atrocities attributed to them. Antoine Court was responsible for renouncing violence and reestablishing Reformed churches on sound footing in 1715. His *Histoire des troubles des Cévennes ou de la guerre des camisards sous le règne de Louis le Grand* (*History of the Troubles of the Cévennes or the War of the Camisards during the Reign of Louis the Great*) in 1760 united oral and written witnesses to counter his prejudices and those of others concerning the Camisard phenomenon. In his magisterial work, he challenged Catholic and Protestant claims and brought the Camisards to life with the excesses of their passions and the courage of their religious convictions.

The uprising of peasants against one of the most powerful European kings had both heroic and heartbreaking aspects. The longevity of the Camisard epic is sustained by the novelty of their combat and sacrifice. They fought despite the odds against them and lived and died with the conviction that their consciences must be free. The exclusion from society and the exile of tens of thousands of Protestants hardened antagonisms for the next century. Despite his boast of reducing the number of Protestants, Louis XIV failed to destroy the Reformed religion in France, and the persecution and exile of Protestants blessed other nations in extending Reformation teachings throughout the world to places of refuge.

In the end, the Camisard insurrection was defeated, and its leaders were executed or exiled. Was the war inevitable? Was it

---

13. Dubled, "Protestants français et l'étranger," 427–28.

THE WAR OF THE CAMISARDS (1702–1704)

unavoidable? What did it accomplish? The Camisards might be excused if they did not follow the Sermon on the Mount. Their adversaries had leveled their temples twenty years earlier in the name of the *Roi Très Chrétien* (Most Christian King), Louis XIV. They had seen their villages go up in flames, the throats of their loved ones slit, their daughters molested and whipped. From their hatred sprang their revulsion and their courage in the face of death. This is their tragic and heroic story.

CHAPTER 2

Reformation and Repression

The War of the Camisards must be understood within the larger context of French religious history beginning with the Protestant Reformation of the sixteenth century. Multitudes embraced the teachings of Martin Luther (1483–1546) and John Calvin (1509–64). Their followers were called Lutherans and Reformed, the latter known as Calvinists and Huguenots. The time seemed opportune for religious change. The kings of France had sought to weaken the control of the Roman Church;[1] the nobility was disgruntled over the privileges enjoyed by the clergy and nourished a hidden hostility that needed only a spark to explode. Among the clergy were eminent prelates who desired reform and priests wearied by the hierarchy's heavy yoke. Yet no one foresaw the terrible combats and persecution that would soon rage with the arrival of the Reformation in France where neither the king nor princes or bishops in great numbers were won over to the Reformed faith.[2]

---

1. The Gallican wing of the French Church sought greater autonomy from the Holy See; the Ultramontane faction supported the traditional position of the absolute authority of the pope (*Petit Robert*, 1125, 2652).

2. Cottret, *Histoire de la Réforme Protestante*, 128.

The War of the Camisards (1702–1704)
FAILED REFORM

The early Reformers did not envision creating a new religion. They held to apostolic teaching that they believed had been corrupted by the Roman Church. They sought a reform of the church, a return to the true Catholic Church, not a new religion. Several attempts in the early 1500s were made to reform the Catholic Church from within. One of the most notable efforts took place under Marguerite of Navarre (1492–1549), a French princess and later queen of Navarre through her marriage to Henry d'Albret of Navarre. She was influenced by the Christian humanism of Erasmus and supported reform efforts in the Catholic Church. Marguerite was the sister of King Francis I (1494–1547), the mother of Huguenot leader Jeanne d'Albret (1528–72), and the grandmother of Huguenot warrior Henry of Navarre (1553–1610), who converted to Catholicism in 1593 to become King Henry IV, the first Bourbon king of France.

Marguerite belonged to a group of Catholics influenced by the Renaissance who adopted Reformation teachings yet remained loyal to the Catholic Church. She discretely supported the Reformers and a group called the Circle of Meaux that included the humanist scholar Jacques Lefèvre d'Étaples, Bishop Guillaume Briçonnet, and William Farel.[3] They were committed to preaching the gospel of justification by faith and opposed the veneration of the saints and the sale of indulgences. In 1521 Lefèvre was appointed to lead reform efforts in Briçonnet's diocese. He translated the Gospels into French, which were distributed throughout the countryside.[4]

When Marguerite established herself at Nérac, the city became a refuge for those persecuted by the Catholic Church. Nicolas Cop, rector of the Sorbonne, was forced to flee Paris for Nérac in 1533 after his evangelical sermon on All Saints' Day. Calvin was suspected of being behind the message and fled with him to find refuge in Nérac with Clément Marot and Lefèvre. Under

---

3. Bayrou, *Henri IV*, 37–39.
4. Stéphan, *Épopée huguenote*, 25–26.

their influence, the surrounding cities of Sainte-Foy-la Grande, Bergerac, Agen, Clairac, and finally La Rochelle were soon won over to the Reformed faith.[5] Francis I continued his protection of Marguerite and the Circle of Meaux until the event known as the Affair of the Placards in October 1534. Posters denouncing the Catholic Mass were displayed publicly in several cities and on the door of Francis's bedchamber. After this event, he consented to brutal measures to suppress the heretics with widespread persecution.[6] The massacre of the Waldensians in 1545 opened the way for further carnage encouraged by the pope, the high clergy, the Parliament of Aix-en-Provence, and the ultra-Catholics.[7]

DILEMMA OF SUBMISSION

Once the hope of reform within the Catholic Church was dashed, Protestantism established itself as a confession separate from the Church of Rome. Around the mid-sixteenth century, Protestants were confronted with the dilemma of reconciling two duties of obedience: their duty of obedience to the king of France as subjects and their duty to God as Christians. The foundation for reflection on this issue for French Reformed believers was Calvin's *Institutes of the Christian Religion*, first published in Latin in 1536, with a dedication to King Francis I, and in French in 1541.[8] The *Institutes* was a statement and defense of Protestant beliefs. In his chapter on civil government, the Reformer treated at some length the duty of submission and obedience to governing authorities, even to those "perverse and unworthy of all honor" who are owed the same "great reverence offered to a good king if they had one."[9] Calvin nuanced his exhortations from Acts 5:29 in stating that passive disobedience was permitted by subjects of the king but open and

---

5. Babelon, *Henri IV*, 76.
6. Félice, *Histoire des Protestants*, 45.
7. Pezet, *Épopée des Camisards*, 32.
8. Félice, *Histoire des Protestants*, 50–52.
9. Calvin, *Institution chrétienne*, 475.

violent revolt was not justified. Obedience required an "exception, or rather a rule to observe above all else when obedience [to government authority] deters from obedience to God."[10]

Between 1552 and 1554 Calvin went further in his *Commentary on Acts of the Apostles* in declaring that a king, prince, or magistrate who acts in a way to diminish the glory of God becomes nothing more than an ordinary man. The authority of the king is not violated when one's religion obligates resistance to tyrannical edicts that forbid rendering to Christ and God the honor and worship of which they are worthy. In the evolution of his thought, Calvin expressed the idea of resistance without specifying its nature.[11] Although most historians believe that Calvin never wavered from the teaching of absolute obedience to civil power or advocated active resistance, his preaching was more nuanced in asserting that a king who submitted his subjects to idolatry lost his legitimacy.[12]

In 1559 the Huguenots established a Confession of Faith at their first National Synod in Paris. Theodore Beza (1519–1605) in his *Histoire Ecclésiastique* reported the existence of 2,150 Reformed churches in the early 1560s, a number both disputed and repeated by many historians. Even if the number of churches was inflated to impress the Crown and gain official recognition, the number of Reformed believers reached its peak around this time only to decline in the following decades through war, reconversion to Catholicism, and emigration.[13] The 1559 definitive edition of the *Institutes* in Latin integrated the idea that an impious prince abolishes his authority. Calvin's disciple and successor, Theodore Beza expressed himself on this difficult subject in a similar vein in his *Confession de la foy chrestienne* (*Confession of the Christian Faith*). He invoked the duties of lesser magistrates to resist tyrants acting against the purity of religion.[14]

---

10. Calvin, *Institution chrétienne*, 480–81.
11. Daussy, "Huguenots entre l'obéissance," 52–54.
12. Cottret, *Histoire de la Réforme Protestante*, 184.
13. Benedict and Fornerod, "2,150 'églises' réformées," 529–30.
14. Bèze, *Confession de la foy chrestienne*, 236.

HOUSES OF GUISE AND BOURBON

This reorientation of Beza's thought might be connected to the Guises and their influence over King Francis II (1544–60) after the death of his father Henry II (1519–59). The House of Guise was an ardent protector of Catholicism and became the archenemies of Protestants. Henry's accidental death in a jousting accident dashed the Huguenots' hope for an edict to obtain legal existence in the kingdom. Francis II's wife was Mary Stuart, Queen of Scots, daughter of James V of Scotland and Marie of Guise. Two of Marie's brothers were French cardinals and her brother Francis was the Duke of Guise. The Guises took control of the government and pushed Francis II "to refuse any compromise with his Reformed subjects." In effect, these initiatives provided the Huguenots with a political cause to exploit. Although the repression came from the king or his entourage, his evil counselors were held responsible for the actions, and the king was considered their prisoner. The idea that the king was the prisoner of the Guises permitted the Huguenots to "reaffirm absolute obedience to the sovereign against whom their successive revolts would however apparently be directed."[15]

The royal House of Bourbon was kept from any influence at the Court and edicts were published calling for the extermination of the Protestant heretics. Each *Parlement* was instructed to send heretics to the stake. Protestants in major cities were arrested and their possessions confiscated. Nobles who came to the Court to reclaim lost lands were turned away by the cardinal of Lorraine, brother of Francis of Guise.[16] Huguenot nobles plotted to kidnap Francis II in March 1560 to remove the king from under the influence of the House of Guise. Calvin condemned the Conspiracy of Amboise because it was not undertaken by *princes du sang* (princes of the royal blood) like Antoine de Bourbon who might have conferred legitimacy to the endeavor. When the plot failed, the ringleader of the conspiracy was killed in the Château-Renault

---

15. Daussy, "Huguenots entre l'obéissance," 58.
16. Félice, *Histoire des Protestants*, 99–101.

forest four days after the abortive attempt. His co-conspirators were hunted down and massacred without due process. Catherine de' Medici (1519–89), widow of the defunct Henry II and now queen regent, was shocked by the savagery of the reprisals against the conspirators and realized that the unity of the kingdom was threatened.

In the aftermath of the conspiracy over a thousand conspirators were executed. There were indications of collusion between the conspirators and the princes of the royal blood but no solid evidence to indict them. Louis de Bourbon, Prince of Condé (1530–69), a descendant of Louis IX (1214–70) and the founder of the House of Condé, was called before the king to defend himself.[17] He was indignant that anyone would suspect him and offered to duel those who accused him. Nonetheless, he was forced to leave the Court and the Guises remained masters of the terrain.[18] The rivalry for the throne between the Guises and the Bourbons lasted for decades and intensified when the Valois dynasty ended with the assassination of Henry III in 1589. For forty years the Guises were the true heads of the Catholic party. Without them, the Reformed religion might have become dominant in France.[19] The failed conspiracy and the repercussions were harmful to the Protestant cause. From then on, many Catholics considered the Huguenots seditious enemies of the kingdom who needed to be exterminated. Many Protestants, convinced of their loyalty to the Crown and persuaded of the justice of their cause, considered the executed conspirators martyrs and sought vengeance.[20]

After the Conspiracy of Amboise, Protestants sought to reconcile their two duties of obedience. When the Wars of Religion inevitably broke out in 1562, French Protestants grounded their conception of obedience in a body of teaching that contained some ambiguity. Their position was radicalized with the Saint

---

17. There was a later Louis II de Bourbon (1621–86), known as the "Grand Condé" for his military victories.

18. D'Aas, *Jeanne III d'Albret*, 241.

19. Félice, *Histoire des Protestants*, 88–89.

20. Stéphan, *Épopée huguenote*, 91.

Bartholomew's Day massacre in 1572. What was clear was the obligation to obey those in authority as long as they did not command disobedience to God.[21] These seminal ideas on resistance are important to understand to explain the War of the Camisards against an "impious king."

---

21. Daussy, "Huguenots entre l'obéissance," 56–57.

CHAPTER 3

War and Broken Treaties

Beginning with the reign of Charles IX (1550–74) in 1560, the monarchy, under the influence of Catherine de' Medici, made attempts toward confessional conciliation. Catherine was now in a position to maneuver between the Bourbons and the Guises. She lent her support to the Reformation by permitting Admiral Gaspard de Coligny (1519–72), the Princess of Condé, and nobles to hold prayer meetings in their apartments at Fontainebleau.[1] She also wanted a moderate in government as an advocate for reconciliation and suggested that the king appoint Michel de L'Hospital (1505–73),[2] a former member of the Parlement of Paris. The eighteenth-century biographer Louis-Jean Levesque de Pouilly regarded L'Hospital as "one of the most esteemed persons that France produced for whom the public good was always the object of his ambitions. L'Hospital desired to make his fellow citizens happier by making them more reasonable."[3] He became chancellor of France on May 6, 1560, and remained in this position until September 27, 1568, during the first (1562–63) and second (1567–68) wars of religion.[4]

1. Stéphan, *Épopée huguenote*, 99.
2. Also spelled L'Hôpital.
3. Pouilly, *Vie de Michel de L'Hôpital*, 1.
4. Galand-Willemen and Petris, *Michel de L'Hospital*, 9.

Upon his appointment as chancellor, L'Hospital supported the Queen Mother in seeking to counter-balance the power of the Guises. He has been described as a man of stoic wisdom living during a time of woe who sought the reconciliation of men with God. If the monarchs of France had adopted his views, the nation might have been spared the wars of religion that raged for two centuries.[5] Although L'Hospital never converted to the Reformed religion, he worked tirelessly for peace between competing confessions, preferring persuasion to constraint, and advanced the concept of the separation of the state and religion to free the nation from unending religious conflicts.[6] In 1560, at the Estates-General, the chancellor affirmed his desire to relegate the terms *Huguenots*, *papists*, and *Lutherans* to the past and conserve only the name *Christian*.[7] The Colloquy of Poissy in 1561, organized by Catherine de' Medici, presented the last opportunity for Catholics and Reformed believers to achieve mutual religious tolerance and national unity. Theodore Beza was present as Calvin's representative along with Reformed lay leaders. The outcome of the colloquy demonstrated the incompatibility of the two faiths particularly on the issue of the Eucharist.[8]

EDICT OF JANUARY

L'Hospital prepared the Edict of January in 1562, assisted by Theodore Beza and Admiral Gaspard de Coligny, which authorized Reformed worship for the first time under certain conditions. The edict offered a ray of hope to the brewing religious tension in France but was rejected by the Catholic Church because it contradicted the Council of Trent that had anathematized Protestant heresies. In provinces dominated by Protestants, Catholics did not

---

5. Crouzet, *Sagesse et le malheur*, 16.
6. Babelon, *Henri IV*, 445.
7. The Estates-General (*États-Généraux*) was an assembly convened by the king composed of the three estates of pre-revolutionary France: clergy, nobility, and commoners (*Petit Robert*, 942).
8. Cottret, *Histoire de la Réforme Protestante*, 183.

THE WAR OF THE CAMISARDS (1702–1704)

understand the attitude of royal authority toward a competing religion. Now the objects of persecution, Catholics awaited the return of the Guises and met violence with violence, and Protestants were executed for the first time since Catherine de' Medici's arrival to power.[9]

After Francis of Guise instigated the massacre of Huguenots gathered for worship in Vassy on March 1, 1562, war became inevitable. Condé raised an army and his capture of the cities of Orléans and Rouen marked the beginning of the Wars of Religion. He justified his actions in responding to the offensive actions of a triumvirate—the Duke of Guise, Duke of Montmorency, and Marshal Saint-André. In his *Déclaration*, Condé proclaimed that the king was not responsible for violating the Edict of January and had no desire to deprive Reformed believers of their freedom of conscience. In his eyes, the fault lay squarely at the feet of the triumvirate who had taken control of the king. Far from an act of disobedience, the action of the Huguenots became a combat to free the king from his captivity.[10]

The massacre of Huguenots at Toulouse and the destruction of churches in Vendôme and Meaux aggravated religious tensions. The Edict of Amboise on March 18, 1563, ended the first war of religion, the nation experienced a brief period of calm, and religious detainees were released. The edict tolerated the freedom of conscience but did not grant freedom of religious worship.[11] After the first war of religion, Catherine organized a vast voyage from 1564 to 1566 to save the kingdom from civil war. King Charles IX had reached his majority and it was time to further his education and display his military power. Along with the king in the elaborate procession were his brothers, Henry and Francis, his sister Marguerite of Valois, his mother, Catherine, and the young Henry of Navarre, the future Henry IV. Religious tensions continued to smolder and Condé provided leadership for the military operations of Huguenot forces in 1567. In November the Battle

---

9. Miquel, *Guerres de religion*, 226–27.
10. Daussy, "Huguenots entre l'obéissance," 58–59.
11. Babelon, *Henri IV*, 94.

of Saint-Denis ended with a Huguenot defeat and the death of the commander of the royal army, the constable de Montmorency. The Peace of Longjumeau in March 1568 confirmed the Edict of Amboise with some additional concessions made to Huguenot nobles to freely worship in their private dwellings.[12]

The third war of religion ended with the Peace of Saint-Germain-en-Laye in 1570. The treaty was negotiated by Catherine de' Medici and Jeanne d'Albret who arranged a marriage between Catherine's daughter Marguerite of Valois and Jeanne's son Henry of Navarre. The marriage took place with great pomp on August 18, 1572.[13] Four days later, on August 22, an attempt was made on the life of the Huguenot leader and military commander Admiral Gaspard de Coligny. Coligny was wounded, and during his recovery on the morning of August 24, 1572, assassins led by the Duke of Guise murdered Coligny and threw his lifeless body out a window. The Saint Bartholomew's Day massacre radically modified the relations between the Huguenots and the king. With the suspected complicity of Charles IX and his mother, Catherine, thousands of his Reformed subjects were murdered in Paris and the provinces as the massacre continued for three days. The Catholic populations of many cities joined in the butchery to extinguish the entire Protestant movement. Henry of Navarre was spared upon his promise to convert to Catholicism.[14]

With the king's determination to persecute the Huguenots, the former argument of manipulation by counselors was no longer valid. From then on the king was seen as a tyrant who persecuted his subjects for their religion. The Huguenots took up arms in active resistance against the sovereign himself. The Edict of Beaulieu in May 1576 under King Henry III granted Huguenots the right to public worship, resulting in the formation of the Catholic League in defense of the Catholic cause led by Henry, Duke of Guise. When Francis, Duke of Anjou, died in 1584 during the reign of his brother Henry III, his cousin Henry of Navarre became the

---

12. Stéphan, *Épopée huguenote*, 133.
13. Babelon, *Henri IV*, 122–23.
14. De Waele, "Cadavre du conspirateur," 97.

legitimate heir to the throne. The interests of the Huguenots turned to defending his right to the crown.[15]

HENRY OF NAVARRE

Henry of Navarre had been raised in the Reformed faith by his mother, Jeanne d'Albret, after her public confession of faith on Christmas Day in 1560. Under his father's influence, he converted to Catholicism in 1562 and returned to the Reformed confession after his father's death that same year. Henry III outlawed the Reformed religion in July 1585, invalidating Navarre's succession to the crown. Pope Sixtus V declared Navarre a heretic and excommunicated him. During the years 1588 and 1589, Navarre multiplied military activity in Normandy and around Paris. Henry III drew closer to Navarre after Henry's rupture with the Catholic League and the assassination by the king's bodyguard in 1588 of Henry of Guise, the leader of the Catholic League and lieutenant general of the king's army. In turn, Henry III was assassinated at Saint-Cloud in August 1589 at the hands of a Dominican monk. Before his death, Henry III implored Navarre to convert to Catholicism and recognized him as his successor.[16]

The Huguenot leader Henry of Navarre converted to Catholicism to end decades of bloodshed and exercise his claim to the throne. He was crowned Henry IV in 1594 and the Wars of Religion ended with the Edict of Nantes in 1598. The edict imposed religious co-existence, although Protestants did not obtain full religious freedom or equality with the Catholic Church. The edict was more favorable to the Catholic Church with limitations placed on Protestant worship and authorized only in places where it existed in 1597. Royal texts until this time had referred to Protestantism as the new religion (*nouvelle religion*). In the preamble to the Edict of Nantes, they now belonged to the So-Called Reformed

---

15. Daussy, "Huguenots entre l'obéissance," 61–62.
16. Petitfils, *Assassinat d'Henri IV*, 43–44.

Religion (*la Religion Prétendue Réformée*) with the king's wish that these subjects would return to the true religion, now his own.[17]

Modern historians have generally lauded Henry IV for sacrificing his religious scruples and adopting the religion of the majority of French people to end the interminable civil wars. He survived multiple plots and attempts to assassinate him before falling at the hands of a Catholic zealot on May 14, 1610. With his death, the Protestant cause lost its greatest protector, and his murder strengthened an absolute monarchy. The crime of *lèse-majesté* reinforced the will to elevate kings to a sacred and inviolable place and supported the doctrine of divine right (*droit divin*).[18] The throne was placed so high that to disobey the king was tantamount to disobeying God. The slightest threat to kings in the seventeenth and eighteenth centuries led to ruthless repression.[19]

LOUIS XIII

After Henry's death, his son Louis XIII (1601–43) began to undermine the Edict of Nantes. With the fall of La Rochelle in 1628 and the disappearance of the Protestant political party, Protestants lost their strongholds. After the Peace of Alès (Edict of Grace) in 1629, it became clear that the implementation of the edict depended solely on the will of the king. The enormous numerical imbalance between Protestants and Catholics left Protestants in a position of weakness. From 1629 to 1643, Reformed believers enjoyed periods of security even as Catholic lawyers profited from the flaws of the Edict of Nantes to reduce their rights. At their own expense, Protestants were forced to lodge royal troops and endure attempts to convert them. Yet they did not experience widespread systematic persecution and had the right to appeal before courts of justice to

---

17. *Religion Prétendue Réformée* or R.P.R. was a pejorative designation for the Reformed faith used in various edicts of pacification. Reformed Protestantism was the "So-Called" or "Falsely Called" Reformed Religion.

18. The *droit divin* is the principle by which God designates the king and which serves as the foundation of his sovereignty (*Petit Robert*, 789).

19. Petitfils, *Assassinat d'Henri IV*, 276.

The War of the Camisards (1702–1704)

settle conflicts. Rarely did they win, but they considered the Edict of Nantes irrevocable. They were persuaded that their loyalty to the Crown was a guarantee of their protection by the king from the attacks of Catholic bishops. This illusion would prove itself fatal.

LOUIS XIV

The young King Louis XIV (1638–1715), grandson of Henry IV, came to the throne after the death of Louis XIII in 1643. He continued his father's policies, eventually leading to armed resistance against the monarchy. Initially Cardinal Mazarin, like his predecessor Cardinal Richelieu, managed to maintain the privileges Protestants enjoyed to live and worship differently despite Catholic public opinion. Over time, by bribes, forced conversions, and exile, Protestants were reduced in number, influence, and ability to resist oppression. Where Protestants were in the minority they kept a low profile. Where they were in the majority, as in the diocese of Nîmes, life was not always easy for Catholics.[20]

Louis XIV was the *Roi-Soleil* (Sun King), whose glory and fame radiated throughout Europe. So great was his reign that Voltaire titled a book *Le Siècle de Louis XIV* (*Louis XIV's Century*). For Voltaire, Louis XIV occupied the fourth great century of human history; the first century was that of Alexander, Aristotle, and Plato; the second of Caesar Augustus, Cicero, and Virgil; the third was the end of the Byzantine Empire with the fall of Constantinople by the Ottoman Empire in 1453. Louis XIV was a warrior king whose armies engaged the powers of his day, with remarkable success early in his reign, with stunning defeats later in his reign, and years of misery for his people provoked by a financial and economic crisis. Early in his reign, Louis XIV engaged in his first wars to establish his position as monarch, a strategy influenced by Cardinal Mazarin. The wars toward the end of his reign were

---

20. Crété, *Camisards*, 16.

primarily defensive with the greatest army Europe had known since the Romans.[21]

Two of his latter wars, the War of the Grand Alliance (1689–97) and the War of Spanish Succession (1701–14) took place following the Revocation of the Edict of Nantes and the latter during the War of the Camisards. The War of Spanish Succession was the longest and most difficult during the reign of Louis XIV. The Austrian emperor, the English queen, Holland, Spain, and Portugal opposed him. The king's troops fought on several fronts, and he needed interior unity in his kingdom to combat the peril from outside. At this critical moment when Louis XIV was staring into the abyss, he was faced with an unexpected domestic rebellion in Languedoc that immobilized his troops far from the borders he was defending.[22]

21. Voltaire, *Siècle de Louis XIV*, 1–3.
22. Bosc and Allier, "Guerre des Camisards," 343.

CHAPTER 4

Protestantism Outlawed

The Reformation in France had greatly succeeded in the poorer and more remote southern provinces of Languedoc and Dauphiné, leading to a religious and social revolution. Preaching and Bible translation were in French, and even the illiterate were profoundly marked by the Scriptures, particularly the Old Testament. The conversion to the Reformed faith of large swaths of the population broke the grip of superstitions so dense in rural areas. Mothers and grandmothers exchanged popular children's bedtime songs for Old Testament Psalms of Theodore Beza and Clément Marot (1496–1544).[1]

LANGUEDOC

Languedoc was a province of geographical contrasts united by the Occitan language (*langue d'oc*) rather than the *langue d'oïl* spoken in northern provinces. The province was divided into several regions, including Haut-Languedoc, with Toulouse as the capital, and Bas-Languedoc, where the Reformation developed deep roots in the Cévennes and where most uprisings took place, a mountainous region with three prominent peaks—Esperou, Aigoual, and

---

1. Crété, *Camisards*, 34.

Lozère. The geography of the region, with its mountains, valleys, and rivers, contributed to the success of the Camisards in battle and made confrontations between large armies impossible. As a bastion of Protestantism, Languedoc was treated with an inflexible severity during the reign of Louis XIV.[2] This region also had fewer Protestants flee the kingdom than northern and more prosperous provinces. Forty percent of Protestants in northern provinces of the kingdom crossed the borders to find safety, while only 16 percent in the Midi and 2 percent in the Cévennes fled France.[3]

The beginning of the reign of Louis XIV had signaled a change in royal power toward the Reformed religion. Louis's *Mémoires* in 1661 prefigured the king's intentions and his refusal to accept the cohabitation of two religions in his kingdom. He violated the rights of the Huguenots and at the Court "did not permit dissent among the nobility to prevent any factions to choose a leader."[4] The presence of Reformed churches tarnished the kingdom and weakened the glory of the king. On the day of his coronation, the king had sworn to extirpate heresy and bring Protestants back to the Catholic Church, not only because it was the only true religion but it was essential for national unity. There was also an aversion toward the Presbyterian ecclesiology of Reformed churches and synods with hints of republicanism. Due to political necessities and "a time of war with England," Louis XIV did not initially openly attack the Reformed religion.[5]

Louis XIV preferred to allow the Reformed religion to die a slow, suffocating death through legal proceedings and the development of missions to convert the Huguenots. He was incited against the Reformed confession by "the complaints of the clergy, the insinuations of the Jesuits, the Roman court, and by Chancellor Tellier and his son Louvois... who wanted Reformed believers to die as rebels."[6] Temples were destroyed on the slightest pretext.

---

2. Pezet, *Épopée des Camisards*, 11–12.
3. Garrisson, *Histoire des Protestants*, 193–95.
4. Dreyss, *Mémoires de Louis XIV*, ccxxxiv.
5. Dreyss, *Mémoires de Louis XIV*, 78–79, 206.
6. Voltaire, *Siècle de Louis XIV*, 413–14.

The War of the Camisards (1702–1704)

Protestant men were not allowed to marry Catholic women, and priests sought ways to remove children from Protestant homes. Money was offered to those who converted to Catholicism, and proselytism was reserved for the Catholic clergy alone.

ENGLAND AND POLITICAL EXPEDIENCY

Two exterior events, the English Revolution and the execution of King Charles I (1600–1649) in 1649, brought considerable prejudice to French Protestants. It did not escape the notice of anyone in France that Protestants had executed the English king. Understanding the danger, Huguenots loudly expressed their disapproval. Because Cardinal Mazarin needed England in the interminable war with Spain, and to remain in the good graces of Oliver Cromwell, Mazarin made an effort to treat Protestants with favor. However, once he was assured of the alliance with England, the cardinal hurried to enact repressive measures against Protestants and permanently suppressed their national synods. The king authorized them to hold a general synod in November 1659 at Loudun, where the king's representative reproached the Huguenots for their insolence and announced that this would be their last general synod. An order was later given that required a Catholic royal commissioner at provincial synods. Contrary to the Edict of Nantes, these measures were attempts to dismantle Protestant churches. Huguenots thought they had found an ally when the English monarchy and the Church of England were restored in 1660 under the Protestant king Charles II (1630–85). To their dismay, Charles II was an admirer of Louis XIV, and the English king treated Protestants outside the Church of England unfavorably.[7]

CONVERSION TO CATHOLICISM

In the entourage of Louis XIV, the passage from Calvinism to Catholicism was easily accomplished, and the resistance of others

---

7. Crété, *Camisards*, 17.

Protestantism Outlawed

outside the Court was viewed as pride rather than a problem of conscience. Official declarations and edicts were multiplied to marginalize Protestants and reduce the number of their places of worship. Pastors who preached on the ruins of temples were arrested. Where Protestants were allowed to gather it was forbidden to sing psalms in the streets and public places. If they sang in their homes the windows had to be closed to prevent anyone outside from hearing them. Only twelve people were allowed to attend weddings or baptisms and the time of burials was regulated. Protestants were constrained to observe Catholic holidays, decorate the front of their homes for Catholic processions, and remove their head coverings when the Holy Sacrament passed by. Their schools were closed, and they were excluded from a large number of professions. Their families were undermined when the age of consent was lowered for children to abjure the Reformed religion and embrace Catholicism. In 1665 a decree allowed priests assisted by a judge to be present at the deathbed of Protestants to solicit their abjuration *in extremis*.[8]

The spectacular conversion of Turenne to Catholicism in 1668 in the presence of the archbishop of Paris was followed by many others of the high nobility. Efforts to undermine the Reformed religion then accelerated after 1670.[9] Madame de Maintenon (the second wife of Louis XIV), Père La Chaise (Louis XIV's confessor), Chancellor Le Tellier (Louvois), and the quinquennial assemblies of the Catholic clergy systematically and patiently weakened the influence and position of Protestantism in France. They were powerful and implacable enemies who served a vainglorious absolute monarch. Louis XIV was convinced that the grandeur of his glory required one faith, one law, and one king. The rights of Protestants were successively withdrawn, first political rights, then legal and religious ones. Despite the efforts of the Jesuits, the disintegration of their institutions, legal proceedings against pastors and consistories, the vexations in their professional activities, and obstacles to the practice of their religion, the Huguenots remained firm in

---

8. Crété, *Camisards*, 19.
9. Rosa, "Turenne's Conversion in Context," 632.

their convictions. The proliferation of decrees between 1660 and 1685 showed the difficulty the king's agents encountered in enforcing them. Although pastors reminded their flocks that obedience to God came before obedience to the king, Protestants clearly affirmed their respect and attachment to the monarchy.[10]

To advance the rate of conversions, beginning in 1681 royal troops were lodged (*dragonnades*) in the homes of Protestants in Languedoc.[11] Soldiers were allowed to engage in all manner of cruelty to obtain conversions. They not only burned Bibles and furniture and destroyed barns, but they also beat Protestants with batons, dragged women by the hair, and practiced torture to elicit conversion. The most stubborn had their fingernails, beards, and hair pulled out. Others were attached to ropes and repeatedly raised and lowered into a pit or prevented from sleeping. Although rape and murder were not officially permitted, reports indicate the commission of these crimes against the Huguenots. There were thousands of abjurations and thousands of others fled into exile. The city of Amsterdam offered refuge to any who arrived there. Of those who remained in France, Protestants who tried to return to the Reformed religion after their forced conversions were imprisoned.[12]

PEACEFUL RESISTANCE

Respectful Protestant appeals to the king received no response. When the Huguenot lawyer Claude Brousson (1647–98) saw that legal recourse failed to stop religious repression, he endeavored to draw the king's attention to the plight of Protestants. In 1683 he planned a peaceful gathering of Protestants and met secretly with twenty-eight deputies from the churches of Languedoc. It was decided that in those places where Reformed worship was forbidden,

---

10. Bosc and Allier, "Guerre des Camisards," 337.

11. *Dragonnades* were a form of persecution under Louis XIV. Protestants were forced to lodge the king's cavalrymen to induce Protestants to convert to Catholicism (*Petit Robert*, 783).

12. Crété, *Camisards*, 21–22.

Protestants would gather publicly on an appointed day. To avoid a massacre Brousson advised the attendees to come unarmed. He understood the dangers and saw this as the least dangerous course of action. The undertaking failed for several reasons, principally because of the dissension between the reluctant urban elite and the more determined common people from the countryside. Several regions refused to participate in the public manifestation, fearing more repression.

The churches of Haut- and Bas-Languedoc and the consistories of Castres and Nîmes opposed even peaceful resistance. Despite the opposition, the towns and villages of Dauphiné, Vivarais, and the Cévennes seized the opportunity to gather at their dilapidated temples. A few days later, church representatives assembled to declare both their loyalty to the king and their intention to defend the freedom of conscience granted by the Edict of Nantes. Violence broke out in August when Catholics tried to forcibly prevent the public celebration of Reformed worship. In response, Protestants attempted to recruit thousands of men for armed resistance against their oppressors. The authorities dispatched soldiers, leading to a clash between the royal troops and Protestants. The slaughter and repression were horrific; the king's troops executed fifty men either burned at the stake or by hanging. Two pastors were condemned to be broken on the wheel (*rompu* or *roué vif*), one of the most savage forms of execution ever devised and reserved for the worst criminals. Many pastors fled to Switzerland, where Brousson also found refuge. From there he went to Holland and published a defense of his failed project to remove any misunderstandings about his intentions.[13]

Toward the end of 1684 and early 1685, when Louis XIV had nothing to fear from neighboring nations, his troops were sent into all the cities where Protestants were in the majority. The *dragonnades* intensified with the excesses of undisciplined dragoons. The borders were surveilled to prevent the flight of those who refused to unite themselves with the Catholic Church. Often a bishop or priest marched at the head of the soldiers. Voltaire notes

13. Crété, *Camisards*, 22–25.

THE WAR OF THE CAMISARDS (1702–1704)

the strange contrast between a Court where the graces and charms of society reigned and the harsh and pitiless orders issued from it. "Paris and Versailles were not exposed to these vexations. The cries [of Reformed believers] would have been too close to the throne. Let the rebels suffer as long as their cries are not heard."[14]

REVOCATION OF THE EDICT OF NANTES

In 1685, Louis XIV arrived at the summit of his glory, and the Protestants had not disappeared. The coronation of James II (1633–1701) in February 1685, England's last Catholic monarch, influenced Louis's decision to finish with the Protestant question once and for all. Since the forced lodging of soldiers in Protestant homes had succeeded in Poitou and Dauphiné, the king decided to send them to convert other provinces. The *dragonnades* commenced in Béarn, and the terrorized population abjured in mass. The king's intendant gave assurance of the total conversion of Béarn. The success was repeated in Normandy, La Rochelle, Montpellier, Nîmes, and many other places where Protestants, terrified by accounts of the *dragonnades*, abjured at the approach of the soldiers.[15]

Louis XIV was led to believe that through conversion to Catholicism, the number of Huguenots diminished to the point where the Edict of Nantes was no longer needed. In reality, there were still nearly a million Protestants in the kingdom in 1685. At the height of his power, he outlawed the Protestant religion with a stroke of his pen in 1685 with the Revocation of the Edict of Nantes. Pastors were ordered to either renounce their faith or leave the kingdom, and emigration was forbidden under pain of death, life sentence on the king's galleys, or imprisonment. Despite the interdiction to emigrate, thousands fled and found refuge in Protestant nations. Those who remained were subject to strict observance of the Catholic religion. In regions of the kingdom

---

14. Voltaire, *Siècle de Louis XIV*, 416–17.
15. Crété, *Camisards*, 25–26.

Protestantism Outlawed

where Huguenots were concentrated, particularly Languedoc and the Cévennes, there was mounting resistance to the royal edict.[16] Prior to the Revocation, "Despite long years of rivalry and bloody conflict, Huguenots and Catholics living in confessionally mixed communities intermarried, sponsored each others' children at baptism, worked together, shared civic responsibility, and participated in each others' observances."[17] Now they once again became enemies. Huguenots could no longer employ Catholics for fear they might convert to Protestantism. Catholics were ordered to release Huguenot domestic servants in order for the authorities to arrest them as vagabonds. "There was nothing consistent in the manner to persecute them, except the intention to oppress them until they converted."[18]

The Articles of the Revocation ordered the demolition of Protestant temples, forbade all religious assemblies with the threat of prison, ordered the expulsion within fifteen days of all Protestant pastors who refused to convert to Catholicism, outlawed Protestant schools, obliged all infants to be baptized into the Catholic Church, ordered the confiscation of possessions of those who had already emigrated unless they returned within a specified period, forbade Protestant emigration under the threat of galleys for the men and imprisonment for the women, and stipulated punishment for New Converts who refused the sacraments of the Church. The Catholic Church opened centers of conversion, and Protestantism no longer had the right to exist in the kingdom.[19] Curiously, the last article allowed those of the So-Called Reformed Religion who remained in the kingdom to privately keep their faith without being troubled until their enlightenment on the condition to not engage in the practice of their religion. There was considerable debate among Catholic leaders on how to treat the New Converts. They also recognized that only two out of a hundred were genuinely converted to the Catholic faith. Some counseled gentle persuasion

---

16. Crété, *Camisards*, 28–29.
17. Luria, "Separated by Death," 185–86.
18. Voltaire, *Siècle de Louis XIV*, 420.
19. Carbonnier-Burkard, *Révolte des Camisards*, 17–19.

to prevent the New Converts from fleeing the kingdom. Others recommended severe measures against the New Converts, forcing them to attend Mass and participate in the sacraments.[20]

From 1685 to 1715 over two hundred thousand Protestants escaped and emigrated to places of refuge, including Geneva, England, Germany, and Holland. Among them were soldiers, sailors, magistrates, intellectuals, merchants, and craftsmen whose departure impoverished France and enriched her neighbors. The majority of those who remained, two-thirds of Reformed believers, did not convert to Catholicism and began to organize themselves, first in small groups and later in large assemblies in out-of-the-way places. Less than a month after the Revocation, the Edict of Potsdam under Frederick William, Elector of Brandenburg and Duke of Prussia, encouraged Protestant refugees to relocate to Brandenburg and granted them the same rights and privileges as those born there.[21]

---

20. Armogathe and Joutard, "Bâville et la consultation," 158–59.
21. Carbonnier-Burkard, *Révolte des Camisards*, 20–22.

CHAPTER 5

Preachers and Prophets

After the Reformed religion was outlawed in 1685, over six hundred Protestant temples were ransacked and destroyed and pastors were exiled. The dreaded *dragonnades* were unexpected, and the arrival of troops caused panic. The Huguenots became metaphoric Hebrews, and their prophets and military leaders adopted names associated with the Jewish people of the Old Testament—*Abraham* Mazel, *Salomon* Couderc, and *Élie* Marion, among others. Huguenots in the Cévennes worshiped and wandered in the woods and savage places of this region. The prophets and preachers of the Cévennes were often painted as subversive rebels working hand-in-hand with France's enemies to deliver the province to foreign powers. They were influenced by the writings of Pierre Jurieu (1637–1713) that were circulated in France. The Catholic historian Brueys attributed the fanaticism to the "inflamed imagination" of Jurieu, who stirred up the provinces from his exile in Rotterdam.[1] Brueys severely criticized the "cowardly pastors who far from giving their lives for the sheep, abandoned them, fled to foreign lands and exhorted them from afar, from a place of security, to hold forbidden assemblies,

---

1. Brueys, *Histoire du fanatisme*, 19.

to revolt, and to sacrifice everything for a religion for which [the pastors] cared little."[2]

From his exile, Jurieu wrote *Lettres Pastorales Addressées aux Fidèles de France Qui Gemissent Sous la Captivité de Babylon* (*Pastoral Letters Addressed to the Faithful of France Who Groan Under the Captivity of Babylon*). In the final month of 1686, rumors circulated that German princes entered into a coalition against Louis XIV and that a war was on the horizon, a war interpreted by many Reformed believers as God's punishment against a kingdom of persecutors. From 1686 to 1700 the rhythm of persecution accelerated. There were 320 condemnations to the king's galleys, mostly Huguenots surprised at illegal assemblies.[3]

BÂVILLE AND CHAILA

Following the Revocation, the Protestants of Languedoc were under the heavy hand of Nicolas de Lamoignon de Bâville (1648–1724).[4] He was placed at the head of an administration in a region almost exclusively Protestant. After the War of the Camisards, he wrote to his brother in 1708, "[I] never agreed with the decision to revoke the Edict of Nantes." He carried out orders and did so with great efficiency.[5] When Louis XIV sent him to Languedoc in 1685, sixty thousand Protestants recanted in three days. Bâville assisted François de Langlade, Abbot du Chaila (1647–1702), in efforts to pacify the Cévennes and return Protestants to the Catholic fold. To accomplish his missionary work, Abbot du Chaila employed torture after his discourses failed. Huguenots sought to flee the region, and when they were caught, the abbot imprisoned them and provided religious instruction in the caverns under his Pont-de-Montvert manor. Bâville despised the Huguenots and considered them guilty of treason and heresy. In his *Mémoires*, he accused

2. Brueys, *Histoire du fanatisme*, 270.
3. Ducasse, *Guerre des Camisards*, 24.
4. Bâville is also spelled "Bâsville."
5. Cazenove, "Portrait de Bâville," 222.

the Huguenots of the sixteenth century of dragging the preserved body of the eleventh-century bishop of Lodeve through the streets of "which a hand remains and a few relics."[6]

Bâville agreed with others that the Huguenots of Alais were "good Huguenots and very bad Christians."[7] He was regarded as the "king of Languedoc" and managed to appoint his brother-in-law Victor-Maurice, Count de Broglie (1647–1727), as commander of the royal troops in Languedoc.[8] Arrests, massacres, and executions increased throughout the region. During the massacre at Coutal, the dragoons killed or wounded over seventy Protestants, and the survivors were placed in stocks. Bâville congratulated the captain and regretted that he had not cut off the noses of the women. He sought to establish peace by filling dungeons with women and sending men to the king's galleys.[9]

In the absence of pastors, prophets and prophetesses proliferated in Dauphiné, Vivarais, and the Cévennes. In the beginning, these self-appointed leaders preached the Bible, exhorted people to repentance, and promised them freedom. They claimed inspiration from the Spirit and were nourished by the Old Testament. Apart from the disconcerting behavior associated with the prophecies, the content of the messages was most often in continuity with the preaching of the seventeenth century. Many fell into mystical trances, and the message turned to armed resistance over time. Most pastors in exile disapproved of their activities and attributed the excesses to the lack of spiritual guides.[10] The Protestant nobility "were certainly attracted to any effort to restore the faith of their fathers [but] they were repelled by the violence and even more by the apocalyptic prophetism of the peasants rebelling in the name of that faith."[11]

6. Bâville, *Mémoires*, 53.
7. Bâville, *Mémoires*, 284.
8. Armogathe and Joutard, "Bâville et la guerre," 45.
9. Ducasse, *Guerre des Camisards*, 26–27.
10. Miquel, *Guerres de religion*, 209–10.
11. Monahan, "Between Two Thieves," 537.

The War of the Camisards (1702–1704)

The first lay preachers, known as *prédicants*, appeared in the Cévennes, Vivarais, and Dauphiné in 1686.[12] They were created spontaneously from a Protestantism fighting for survival. Many Protestants found refuge in the Cévennes, living in caverns, ruined houses, sheepfolds, and forests. The royal authorities considered them fugitives, and Bâville built forts and roads to more easily track them down. However, the Cévennes was a region difficult to monitor and the fugitives, with the complicity of the population, lived there for several years. Their faith grew during this time of suffering. They refused to bow their knee to Baal and saw themselves as the elect children of God.[13] From among them, preachers emerged to reignite the flame of God's word and reestablish family worship, men like Claude Brousson, Fulcran Rey, François Vivent, Jean Manoël, and Isaac Vidal.

The assemblies took place mostly at night in remote places. There they preached, baptized, and observed the Lord's Supper, worshiping in fear of the arrival of the king's soldiers. When the wool comber Isaac Vidal preached for the first time, over two thousand people gathered to hear him. The congregation was exhorted to flee from Babylon, and many vowed never to return to the Mass. Brousson reported that at Vidal's preaching people "threw themselves to the ground, pulled out their hair, broke down in tears, confessed their sins, and implored the mercy of God."[14] Many were arrested and tortured. For the men caught, there was the king's galleys for life or execution. Fulcran Rey was hanged after being tortured. Shortly before his death, he wrote to his father: "Oh how happy would I be if I were among the number of those whom the Lord has reserved to announce his praises and die for his interests."[15] The suffering of these heroes of the faith contributed to the growing numbers of Huguenots gathering for worship.

---

12. The *prédicants* replaced exiled pastors (Bost, *Prédicants Protestants des Cévennes*, 93).

13. Bost, *Prédicants Protestants des Cévennes*, 95–96.

14. Brousson, *Relation Sommaire des Merveilles*, 5.

15. Crété, *Camisards*, 39–40.

MILITIAS AND SPIES

Bâville recognized the dangers of these mass gatherings of Protestants. He organized regiments of civilian militias and constructed three forts for which the king provided cannons to use against the heretics. The militias acted as a national guard composed of Catholics and New Converts who had proven their fidelity to the Church. They were paid by the province and led by *gentilshommes* who had purchased their rank.[16] The capture of fugitives and house searches were conducted by the militias in the absence of regular troops who had been called to defend the kingdom's borders. In the summer of 1688 the Duke of Noailles declared a general disarmament of the population, carrying weapons was forbidden, and all former authorizations were revoked. A decree from the king arrived in October requiring all recent New Converts to hand over their arms and ammunition to the local magistrates, and in November it was added that those in violation would be sentenced to the king's galleys. The few companies of troops left in the province received the order to be pitiless in carrying out the king's orders.

Louvois, the secretary of war, considered Bâville's treatment of the assemblies too weak and ordered the troops to take fewer prisoners and massacre more men and women alike as an example. A system of espionage was established in the region by Bâville and Bishop Esprit Fléchier of Nîmes. He was instructed to choose and pay several men in each locality to spy on their Protestant neighbors and keep them informed of religious activities. The year 1688 ended painfully for the Cévenols. On the night of December 26 an assembly was discovered in a cavern. Two assistants, Jean Pierre Bony and Jacques Puech, were hanged and nine others were sentenced to the galleys. Sixteen women and nine girls were imprisoned in the château of Sommières and one, Suzon de Jean, was taken to the infamous Tower of Constance.[17]

---

16. *Gentilshommes* were nobles attached to the person of the king, a prince, or a grand seigneur (*Petit Robert*, 1146).

17. Bost, *Prédicants Protestants des Cévennes*, 307–8.

THE WAR OF THE CAMISARDS (1702–1704)

The prophetic movement began before the War of the Camisards and profoundly divided Protestantism in France and the *Refuge*.[18] The movement was severely criticized by the upper classes, not least because the phenomenon was largely manifested among poor, young artisans and peasants who were most often illiterate. Pastors in the *Refuge* expressed skepticism of reported miracles and manifested disdainful disapproval toward the "little prophets." The controversy was sharp between ardent defenders of the prophets, Brousson and Jurieu, and those radically hostile, the majority of pastors in the *Refuge*.[19]

ISABEAU VINCENT

In February 1688 in Dauphiné, Isabeau Vincent, a young teenage shepherdess, spoke about the "wonderful things of God" while sleeping. Her godfather tried unsuccessfully to awaken her. With her eyes closed and in a strong voice, she proclaimed a call to repentance. The phenomenon continued, and although she didn't know how to read or write and spoke only in her regional dialect, according to witnesses, she prophesied in French. People from the surrounding area came to hear her exhort, edify, and console her listeners. She brought hope to those who had converted to Catholicism and pronounced judgment on their persecutors. Soon her prophesying was not limited to times of sleeping as she began traveling from place to place. Many of those who heard her, of all ages, sexes, and social positions, began prophesying as well. As might be expected, the authorities did not take long to react. In June, Isabeau was arrested and placed in a convent. Her arrest did not end the occurrence of prophetic activity. Others went throughout the countryside preaching and transmitting the gift of prophecy.

---

18. The *Refuge* refers to the exile of Protestants to countries of safety to escape persecution. The first wave of departures took place after the Saint Bartholomew's Day massacre in 1572. After the Revocation of the Edict of Nantes in 1685 tens of thousands fled France to places where they could freely worship.

19. Chabrol, "Diffusion et filiations," 146.

Preachers and Prophets

At the beginning of 1689, over two hundred young people were allegedly prophesying in their sleep in Dauphiné. Contrary to the preachers who had sought to reconstitute the ancient structures of Reformed churches, the prophets and prophetesses broke with the past.[20]

Prophetism crossed the Rhône to Vivarais and became more violent with new characteristics. Entire assemblies were affected by the "breath of the Spirit." A prophet from the village of Cliousclat purportedly communicated the gift of the Spirit to several women in 1689 and declared that the Holy Spirit had revealed himself throughout Dauphiné. He announced that the Protestant religion would soon triumph in the kingdom of France and in three months the great judgment would take place. The Spirit also spoke of a great battle between the peoples of Europe and Louis XIV leading to the king's defeat. The prophet La Valette, hearing that the king's troops were marching against the faithful, prophesied that the weapons would fall from the hands of the dragoons and turn against them. A few hours later, a captain and nine soldiers were massacred by a roving band of the prophet's followers. Many believed they were invincible and would be resurrected after a few days if killed. In February 1689, the troops of the commander of Vivarais came across an assembly and surrounded it. The prophets assured those present that they had seen guardian angels and that the people had nothing to fear. They rushed to encounter the troops, who massacred over three hundred of them. Others were imprisoned or fled to the mountains. The grand assemblies ceased as Bâville multiplied arrests and executions. In Vivarais and Dauphiné all that remained were occasional solitary prophets and sporadic manifestations of prophetism.[21]

---

20. Crété, *Camisards*, 55–57.
21. Crété, *Camisards*, 58.

CHAPTER 6

Return from Exile

In the first days of 1689, while almost two hundred Reformed believers were imprisoned in the forts of Nîmes and Alais, François Vivent (1664–92) arrived from Holland to Switzerland to prepare his return to France with a letter from Pierre Jurieu. Jurieu had announced that there would be a great deliverance in 1689 from the yoke of oppression. The Glorious Revolution of England in 1688 deposed James II who fled from William III of Orange (1650–1702) and found refuge in France. Jurieu's predictions about divine intervention against the enemies of Protestantism were ridiculed after the Revocation. But now France's borders were threatened, and the Court could not hide its apprehension.[1]

CHURCH OF THE DESERT

Claude Brousson was in exile in Lausanne and was struck by the spiritual void left by the forced exile of pastors after the Revocation. He studied the book of Revelation of the New Testament and found the source for his thunderous warnings and calls to repentance for Protestants who had returned to the Catholic Church. Several thousand of his sermon pamphlets were sent to

---

1. Bost, *Prédicants Protestants des Cévennes*, 309.

Languedoc. He entitled his collection of sermons *La manne mystique du désert* (*The Mystical Manna of the Desert*). Despite the danger that awaited them, Vivent and Brousson returned to the Cévennes in 1689 to console their oppressed brothers and sisters and address doctrinal errors and practices that had arisen in the absence of pastors.

Vivent had received ordination while in exile and became pastor of the Church of the Desert. The Church of the Desert recalled the wilderness wanderings of the children of Israel after their exodus from Egyptian bondage and came to designate the period when the Reformed religion was outlawed. The church was mostly composed of the lower classes of society—artisans, sheep and goat herders, and farmers. When Brousson and Vivent arrived in the Cévennes they called an assembly and organized a day of fasting and repentance. Amazed at the people's zeal, they were persuaded that by taking up arms they could serve God and hasten the deliverance of the true church. These men were united in their desire to reestablish Protestant worship and were bound by the conviction that state-authorized religion was not in conformity with biblical teachings.[2]

Vivent consecrated Brousson to the pastoral ministry before they separated to minister in different regions, Vivent to Bas-Languedoc and Brousson to the Cévennes, where he became the most famous clandestine preacher. There Brousson wandered from place to place, traveled great distances, and held assemblies to instruct and comfort his people. Through his social origin and professional training, Brousson was by far the most educated and qualified to lead in reestablishing the ruined structures of Reformed churches. He wrote out the sermons of others with an apocalyptic emphasis. The image of the desert, a place of trials and suffering, was prominent in his messages and used to understand the evils experienced by God's people.

Brousson also intended to join the coalition of William of Orange in the hope of fomenting an insurrection. He and Vivent were in regular contact with friends in Switzerland and government

---

2. Crété, *Camisards*, 41–43.

THE WAR OF THE CAMISARDS (1702-1704)

leaders in England and Holland to request foreign intervention. A price was put on both their heads by Bâville, the king's steward.[3] Vivent had thought often about the hour of his death, knowing that if he fell into the hands of the enemy, a cruel death by torture awaited him. He was killed in a cavern defending himself in February 1692 but not before killing several attackers. His body was dragged through the streets of Alais face down against the ground with the words "traitor and assassin" attached to the wagon; his body was burned and his ashes thrown to the wind. His four companions were captured and hanged.[4]

After Vivent's death, Brousson remained the only leader of the Church of the Desert. Over time, however, his perspective on the means to accomplish divine purposes evolved from armed confrontation to spiritual resistance. When the army of the Duke of Schomberg penetrated into Dauphiné in the summer of 1692, Protestants saw their deliverance. Brousson's pacifism prevented the Cévenols from sharing their co-religionists' enthusiasm, and the duke's army returned home. Brousson wrote the king to inform him of the people's suffering and wrote Bâville to warn him of imminent divine judgment on France. The king's troops pursued him day and night, and he again found refuge in Holland. Many preachers were captured, yet the resistance and the illegal assemblies multiplied.[5] While Brousson was in Holland, the Treaty of Ryswick in 1697 ended Louis XIV's war against an alliance of England, Holland, and Austria. Rumors circulated that the French king was prepared to offer clemency to Protestants and allow them to gather for worship in their homes, bury their dead in public cemeteries, have their marriages blessed, and permit his subjects to practice the religion of their choice. In truth, the king had not consented to any of these measures. Brousson returned to Languedoc in 1698 where the *dragonnades* of the king's troops had restarted in the homes of Protestants.[6]

3. Crété, *Camisards*, 44-46.
4. Bost, *Prédicants Protestants des Cévennes*, 466-68.
5. Crété, *Camisards*, 47-48.
6. Ducasse, *Guerre des Camisards*, 49-50.

TERROR AND EXECUTIONS

With Protestants facing increased persecution, France had become a place of desolation, and a new wave of terror struck the Cévennes. Soldiers went house to house searching for weapons and heretical books. Those found in possession of them were condemned to fines or the king's galleys. People were forcefully escorted to Mass by soldiers and fined for refusing to send their children to catechism. Brousson finally realized that the king, not the provincial governors, was responsible for the persecution. With this conviction, he once again wrote the king a series of petitions and sent them to other provinces and countries to influence public opinion. The king's intendant distributed his portrait throughout Languedoc. Brousson was recognized, arrested, and imprisoned, then escorted to Montpellier to stand in judgment. Brousson admitted the charges against him, that he had preached throughout the province, held communion services, and baptized infants. When asked why he had returned to France, he replied, "To console my brothers." He was condemned to be broken on the wheel and strangled to prevent him from speaking. Before he died he sent a note to the judge disavowing participation in violent actions. According to a witness, Brousson walked to his execution as if going to a feast. He was executed as an enemy of the state. He was celebrated as a martyr of the faith.[7]

While in Vivarais and Dauphiné the prophetic movement ceased, in the Cévennes and Bas-Languedoc prophetism arrived like a flood. The first Cévenol inspirations were similar to those of Vivarais and Dauphiné marked by an invitation to individual conversion and a return to the evangelical faith.[8] During the summer of 1700, an old woman began prophesying in the diocese of Uzès. She was accompanied by a farmer, Daniel Roux, who also possessed the gift. On their passage, a religious fever took hold of people. The villagers broke down in tears as their bodies shook. Others ran through the streets calling people to repent. There were

7. Crété, *Camisards*, 49–51.
8. Joutard, *Camisards*, 88.

The War of the Camisards (1702–1704)

reports of people crying tears of blood. Élie Marion believed he had been taken to heaven. Witnesses testified that the prophets all spoke in good French using the same phrase, "I tell you, my child," to announce their prophecies.[9]

Bâville wrote to Bishop Fléchier in May 1701 that he took these prophetic sparks seriously and that repression was the only means to extinguish them. His methods poured oil on the fire and the Cévenols responded with vengeance. At the end of May, a young shepherdess was arrested who claimed to have seen God and angels. The young son of a notary, Jacques Bouton, was also arrested after entering into a trance and prophesying against the kingdom and the Catholic Church. As they were being led to prison, the enraged population delivered them. Armed with axes, they stormed the church, broke the tabernacle holding the Eucharist, turned the altar over, and threw the crucifix to the ground. Bouton was captured and broken on the wheel. In June an entire village rose up against the priests and a judge to deliver an *inspiré* and ransacked the church.[10]

A new wave of terror fell on Languedoc, and repression was followed by calls for Protestants to kill Catholic blasphemers. In response, Bâville informed the communities that women and girls would be punished as rigorously as men. Children caught at illegal assemblies were beaten, men and women guilty of organizing the assemblies were executed on the gallows or the wheel, and the communities were required to pay fines for illegal assemblies. As Bâville cracked down, more prophets arose. The prisons overflowed with children and adolescents mistreated by soldiers. Physicians were called to examine the young prisoners. After long questioning, they determined that the young captives were neither prophets nor demoniacs, nor fakes, nor ill. They searched for a term to provide some explanation and settled on "fanatic." According to a contemporary, there were over eight thousand fanatics in the Cévennes and Bas-Languedoc.[11]

9. Crété, *Camisards*, 61.
10. Crété, *Camisards*, 63.
11. Crété, *Camisards*, 65.

In autumn the surroundings of Nîmes, Mialet, Lasalle, and other places were won over to prophetism. The assemblies lasted ten to twelve hours. The preacher-prophets who spoke were simple peasants, shepherds, wool combers, bakers, and field laborers. They accosted priests on the streets to call them to repentance. The prophets declared that two hundred people would gather to destroy churches and kill Catholics. A young prophetess, Françoise Bres, preached against the Catholic Eucharist and was arrested by Abbot du Chaila along with a young friend. The young man was sent to the king's galleys, and Françoise was hanged on the gallows on January 24, 1702, at Pont-de-Montvert. The abbot did not have long to live, and his death became the key trigger for the coming war. He lived in opulence in his two-story house next to the church. Even those close to Chaila reproached him for his brutality and thirst for power. Worse, he tortured and executed prisoners in his prison cave. His missionary ardor and police activities made him odious in the eyes of the Huguenots, and he would pay with his life.[12]

---

12. Crété, *Camisards*, 66.

CHAPTER 7

The Sword of Vengeance

The War of the Camisards can be divided into several phases that correspond to the different military leaders of France at the head of royal armies. The first period was under Lieutenant-General Broglie from July 1702 to February 1703 and was marked by the victories of Jean Cavalier and Roland. The second period was under Marshal de Montrevel from February 1703 to March 1704. Montrevel sought to repress the insurrection at any price, incinerated a large part of the Cévennes, deported thousands from their villages, and sowed terror throughout the region. Marshal de Villars replaced Montrevel in the third period from April to December 1704. Villars succeeded in persuading Jean Cavalier to surrender and leave the kingdom. Roland continued his resistance until his betrayal and death in August 1704, after which most Camisard leaders surrendered or were exiled. The fourth period with Marshal Berwick occurred after the war ended from January 1705 to October 1710. It was marked by attempts to revive the insurrection under Abraham Mazel and Pierre Claris. With their executions in 1710, the rebellion was definitively crushed.[1]

---

1. Bosc and Allier, "Guerre des Camisards," 350–52.

The Sword of Vengeance

DEATH OF ABBOT DU CHAILA

After years of executions, imprisonments, separation of families, and corpses dragged through the streets of those who died without receiving the sacraments of Rome, a furious rage seized the mountain people of the Cévennes and their grip tightened on their pitchforks and hunting rifles. They had drunk the cup of bitterness to its dregs.[2] Under the leadership of the wool comber Abraham Mazel (1677–1710), a shift took place from a message of repentance and conversion to one of vengeance. Mazel was about twenty-eight years old when God visited him with the spirit of prophecy in 1701. Several months before taking up arms he claimed he had visions of a garden with seven large, black oxen eating cabbage. Mazel was ordered to chase the oxen from the garden. The Spirit of the Lord told him that the garden represented the Roman Church and the large oxen the priests who devoured the garden. Mazel received several inspirations telling him to take up arms with his brothers to combat the priests and burn down the altars.[3]

In July 1702, Mazel, Salomon Couderc, and Pierre Séguier, known as Esprit, received a divine order for an assembly in the woods near Saint-Julien-d'Arpaon. The following day they were met in the village of Bougès by Jacques Couderc and David Mazaurie, who had been told by the Holy Spirit to find Mazel and his companions.[4] They were joined by twenty villagers armed with pistols, rifles, swords, axes, and scythes and warned by the Spirit to carry out his orders to deliver their brothers imprisoned by Abbot du Chaila. They marched all night and surrounded the presbytery. They forced open the doors, demanded the prisoners be freed, and set the edifice on fire. One of the abbot's valets killed an attacker, which further infuriated the invaders.[5]

The abbot broke his leg trying to escape from a window and, according to Mazel, Esprit Séguier struck the first blow before

---

2. Bosc and Allier, "Guerre des Camisards," 338.
3. Ducasse, *Guerre des Camisards*, 68–69; Joutard, *Camisards*, 92.
4. Crété, *Camisards*, 70–71.
5. Puaux, "Origines, causes et conséquences," 210–11.

The War of the Camisards (1702–1704)

others pierced his body over fifty times to satisfy their vengeance. Those who executed the abbot each had a parent, a fiancé, or a friend to avenge. As the Camisards tell it, the abbot begged for mercy and promised to follow the Camisards, leave his residence, and no longer involve himself in religious matters. Some details might have been embellished by the survivors, yet Séguier and his companions viewed the assassination of the abbot as an act of justice.[6] Emboldened by their success, they set fire to churches in Frugères and Saint-André-de-Lancize and killed the village priests, the first falling from the tower where he had sounded the alarm; the second was mutilated and quickly succumbed to his wounds. Three of the attackers were captured and tortured, Séguier among them, whose right hand was chopped off before he was burned at the stake at Pont-de-Montvert on August 13, singing Psalm 69, "Save me, O God! For the waters have come up to my neck."[7]

Unsurprisingly, the Catholic version of the event differs in some details. The number of Camisard scoundrels, some with dubious morals, increased along with their barbarity. The abbot had time to give absolution to his servants and exhort them to die as good Catholics. One of the soldiers was spared when a prisoner testified of his kindness toward the captives. Three other soldiers escaped by jumping into the river. The abbot was offered his life spared if he chose to serve the Camisards as God's minister. He responded that he would rather die a thousand times than serve as their minister. The Camisards dragged him to a bridge and slowly pierced him fifty-four times with a dagger to increase his suffering.[8]

Both stories of the abbot's death are contradictory and implausible. Chaila was ruthless but he did not lack courage. Years earlier as a missionary in Siam (Thailand) he had resisted torture, and there is no chance that the Camisards would have allowed him to become a minister among them. These two accounts did not serve to exactly relate the event but rather to reinforce the faithful

---

6. Crété, *Camisards*, 72.
7. Joutard, *Camisards*, 105–6; Crété, *Camisards*, 74–75.
8. Joutard, *Camisards*, 98–99.

in describing divine justice on the persecutor of Protestants or the death of the first Catholic martyr. Initially, no special importance was accorded to one more senseless act of inter-religious violence. Bâville himself wrote to the secretary of war that there was no evidence of a general insurrection following the abbot's death. Voltaire consulted the archives of the secretary of war to write his history of Louis XIV and concluded that the abbot provoked the war. However, both Protestant and Catholic historians agree that the abbot's murder ignited the war.[9]

Bâville wrote to the king's minister Michel Chamillart (1652–1721) following the murder of Abbot du Chaila, "Already there are more than seventy killed and twenty executed. I still have fifteen who will be judged with as much severity as possible. More are arrested each day."[10] Soldiers and militiamen searched the countryside day and night, arresting people on any suspicion or denunciation by priests. The soldiers wreaked havoc on the farms and in villages, pillaging provisions and mistreating the inhabitants. Gédéon Laporte (1660–1702), formerly in the king's army, replaced Esprit Séguier as the leader of the discontented and preached holy war and armed resistance to punish the infidels. After decades of persecution, the terrible war of the Cévennes ravaged the region. The fugitives roamed the mountains led by a young man, Salomon Couderc, who served as their pastor. They were joined by Laporte, who advised them to procure weapons from Catholic civilians who had been armed by Bâville and Broglie.[11]

JEAN CAVALIER

Jean Cavalier de Ribaute (1681–1740) joined the rebels and became the general of the Army of the Children of God. He was born into a Protestant family, the son of a shepherd, in Mas Roux near Ribaute, a small hamlet in the Cévennes region. His parents

---

9. Joutard, *Camisards*, 100–105.
10. Puaux, "Dépeuplement et l'incendie," 592.
11. Crété, *Camisards*, 78–79.

The War of the Camisards (1702–1704)

belonged to the New Converts, outwardly professing the Catholic faith while despising its religious ceremonies. Jean's mother secretly instructed him in the Reformed religion and warned him about the teachings he received at the Catholic school he was forced to attend. Five years old at the time of the Revocation, he grew up amid religious persecution and witnessed with horror the arrest of attendees of clandestine assemblies. The men were hanged; the women had their heads shaved and were imprisoned in convents or the Tower of Constance at Aigues-Mortes. At a secret gathering in the woods near Uzès when he was twelve, Jean heard the preaching of Claude Brousson, who had returned to the Cévennes from exile.[12]

As a youth, Jean was unable to hide his disdain for Catholicism, especially after the execution of Brousson in 1698. When the village priest brought civil and criminal charges against Jean, he fled, crossed the Rhône River, and arrived in Geneva in 1701 where he worked as a baker. There he received disturbing news that his parents Antoine and Élisabeth had been arrested, his father imprisoned at Carcassonne and his mother in the Tower of Constance. After hearing that his parents had been freed, he made haste to return to France in 1702 and was reunited with them at Ribaute. His joy was short-lived when upon entering the house he saw that his parents were preparing to leave to attend Mass. He understood that their freedom had been purchased at the price of recanting their faith. His parents, moved by his indignation and ashamed of their abjuration, determined to no longer attend Mass. At the age of twenty-one, the gift of prophecy was reportedly transmitted to Cavalier by Daniel Roux.[13]

In the summer of 1702, Colonel Gaspard de Calvière, Marquis of Saint-Cosme, disarmed the New Converts who relied on their arms for their livelihood in hunting. For a long time he had been despised by the New Converts in the Vaunage in southern France. In 1685 the consistory of Nîmes had given him funds to represent the Reformed religion before the Court. Instead of accomplishing

---

12. Stéphan, *Épopée huguenote*, 265.
13. Crété, *Camisards*, 79.

his mission, he converted to Catholicism and became a zealous persecutor of his former co-religionists. He forced people to attend Mass and imprisoned those who refused. On an August day as Saint-Cosme left Mass at Caylar, *inspirés* were told by the Spirit to kill him. They waited for him on his return home and accosted him in a desolate place. He was unable to draw his pistols and was beaten with rods. Wounded, he was taken to his château, where he died. The authorities sought those guilty of the attack, and one suspect, Pierre Bouzanquet, was arrested and tortured although he denied any involvement. He was broken on the wheel and his body exposed on the road from Nîmes to Montpellier. Justice was efficient and blind. The Camisards sprang into action and their vengeance was terrible.[14]

14. Crété, *Camisards*, 76–77.

CHAPTER 8

Massacres and Retaliation

The Camisards went on the offensive and began to wreak havoc throughout the Cévennes under the leadership of Jean Cavalier, Abraham Mazel, Gédéon Laporte, and Salomon Couderc. Over 50 percent of the Camisard warriors were younger than twenty-five years old, mostly from rural or semi-rural regions. Two-thirds were artisans in textile; one-third were shepherds or farmers. The Protestant nobility was largely absent, while some became active in the repression of their co-religionists. In fact, "from the very beginning of the rebellion, the king to whom they had repeatedly sworn their oath commanded them to defend a church they despised and a faith they could not stomach."[1] The Camisards carried out reprisals against their persecutors, both priests and soldiers. They punished their own who committed murder or acts of depredation, held all things in common, had caverns for hospitals, and often dressed in the garments of defeated enemies. Their numbers at any one time rarely exceeded two thousand men against over twenty thousand royal troops. When victorious they held religious assemblies. When vanquished they found refuge in impenetrable gorges.[2]

---

1. Monahan, "Between Two Thieves," 537.
2. Joutard, *Camisards*, 166.

Other young men were recruited as leaders often with *noms de guerre*—Castanet, Catinat, and Ravanel. Like their troops, the leaders were from the families of peasants or artisans and were all either preachers or prophets. Cavalier's troops grew to seven hundred men in addition to fifty horsemen led by Catinat. They were the most experienced combatants, who had astonishing success against royal troops and inflicted the most destruction. In the mountains and valleys, several troop formations operated separately: Roland, with three to four hundred men in the Basses-Cévennes, often fought alongside Cavalier; Jouany was in the north of Bougès with four to five hundred men; and Castanet maneuvered with a more modest number of troops in the region of Aigoual. The Camisards' wives, sisters, and mothers were often involved in the struggle. Most of them assisted in providing supplies for the combatants at the risk of their own lives. On rare occasions, women wielded the sword. Some were prophetesses like *la Grande* Marie Mathieu, hanged in 1704, or Marie *la Blondine*, captured in 1705 upon her return from exile with her husband Castanet and imprisoned in the Tower of Constance at Aigues-Mortes.[3]

EARLY MILITARY ENCOUNTERS

In response to the growing insurrection, Bâville and Broglie sent the infamous Captain Poul after the rebels. Cavalier and Gédéon Laporte faced off at Champdomergue in an indecisive skirmish against royal troops led by Poul. A month later, Laporte and several of his men were surprised in a ravine near Sainte-Croix and killed, their heads exposed on the bridge of Anduze as a warning to the insurgents.[4] Cavalier and Gédéon's nephew Pierre Laporte, later known as Roland, became the principal leader of the Camisards and led groups of poorly armed peasants for two years in guerrilla warfare against royal troops, burning churches and killing priests and denunciators at Générargues and Mialet. They held frequent

---

3. Ducasse, *Guerre des Camisards*, 94–95.
4. Carbonnier-Burkard, *Révolte des Camisards*, 60–63.

worship gatherings and sang "Let God arise" from Psalm 68 before attacking the enemy with fury. The royal troops often fled at the intonation of the first notes of the Camisard hymn. In response, the Court sent a new military leader with his seasoned troops, Brigadier Julien, known as "The Apostate," a former Protestant and pastor's grandson.[5] His cruelty was expressed in letters to Chamillart. Julien wrote that he was ready to exterminate the scoundrels and if he had his way entire populations would be deported.[6]

Roland was accompanied by Jacques Bonbonnoux, whose mother, wife, and mother-in-law were fervent Huguenots, his wife imprisoned at the Tower of Constance before their marriage. They were married before a Catholic priest in 1701, and his wife died the following year. He understood his wife's death as punishment for his unfaithfulness. In 1703 he joined Roland and remained committed to the cause of freedom of conscience during and after the War of the Camisards.[7] The success of the Camisards was partly due to their knowledge of the rugged countryside with its woods, ravines, and caves. They had the complicity of newly converted Catholics and were feared by traditional Catholics. Another advantage for the Camisards was that the royal troops stationed in Languedoc were not always the best. Broglie repeatedly complained about the poor quality of the troops and the officers. He described the officers as the worst in France. The troops were not trained for guerilla warfare and preferred to pillage or remain in their camps.[8]

The Camisards, armed with scythes and sticks, battled superior forces with confidence that, in life or death, they were victorious and never abandoned by the Lord. Destitute, lacking bread, sleeping in the caves of their mountains, and tracked like wild beasts, they resisted to the death. During periods of rest, they read their Bibles attached by a leather belt to their backs, and "this old book gave to their souls the courage necessary to live as they

---

5. Crété, *Camisards*, 108–9.
6. Puaux, "Origines, causes et conséquences," 216.
7. Bonbonnoux, *Mémoires*, 1–2.
8. Joutard, *Camisards*, 174–76.

lived and die as they died."⁹ A Camisard named Étienne Goût was arrested and broken on the wheel in December 1702. Earlier in his ministry, he had constrained a priest from Bugarel to attend an assembly during which several persons prophesied.¹⁰ When the executioner delivered the coup de grâce, Mazel reported that a stream of blood shot from Goût's mouth and fell like rain on the archers. One day Bâville interrogated de Vilas, one of the few *gentilshommes* who joined the insurrection. Bâville was shocked that a man like him was associated with scoundrels. De Vilas responded, "Ah Monsieur, might it please God that I have a soul as beautiful as theirs."¹¹

The Camisards addressed a letter with their demands to the commander of the royal forces, Count de Broglie. They wrote that they simply wanted the freedoms purchased with the blood of their ancestors and that they were prepared to die rather than renounce their beliefs. They expressed their confidence that the God of mercy had poured out his Spirit on them according to the promise of the prophet Joel and they were constrained to now offer their bodies and possessions in sacrifice for the holy gospel and spill their blood for this just cause. The following month, Broglie pursued two of Cavalier's lieutenants, Abdias Maurel, nicknamed Catinat, and Ravanel, with three companies of mounted troops near Nîmes. Broglie was defeated and Captain Poul was decapitated with his own sword.¹² Gédéon Laporte's death was avenged. The Camisards wrote ironically to their enemies: "The chicken [*poule*] is plucked and trussed. You can come and take it."¹³

While Julien the Apostate pursued Cavalier, Jouany massacred the royal garrison at Genolhac. He returned several days later and destroyed the Dominican convent, sowed terror in the countryside, and slaughtered women and children. The massacres met the disapproval of Abraham Mazel who nonetheless justified them

---

9. Bonbonnoux, *Mémoires*, 3.
10. Crété, *Camisards*, 65.
11. Ducasse, *Guerre des Camisards*, 106–7.
12. Stéphan, *Épopée huguenote*, 267–69.
13. Ducasse, *Guerre des Camisards*, 110.

since the enemy did worse. Colonel de Marcilly retook Genolhac and executed one hundred Protestants. Julien carried out punitive expeditions pillaging and burning houses suspected of assisting the rebels. Seized by a thirst for vengeance, Castanet made the population of Fraissinet-de-Fourques pay for the abuses committed against their Protestant neighbors. The village was burned and more than thirty Catholics were massacred. Catholics and Protestants were caught in an infernal cycle from which they could not escape. The burning rage of the Camisards responded to the cold brutality of Marcilly and Julien.[14]

CATHOLIC RETALIATION

Marshal de Montrevel replaced Count de Broglie at the head of three thousand troops in February 1703. That same month, there was a Catholic mobilization against the Camisards that pitted Catholics against Protestants in another cycle of violence and reprisals. Catholics now passed from defensive to offensive measures. The Catholic Pierre Chabert attacked the village of Chamborigaud one day after Jouany's expedition in the same place. Four hundred Catholics from several villages gathered and carried out a punitive expedition against Chamborigaud without support from royal troops. They burned twenty-seven homes and massacred fourteen New Converts. Military authorities were troubled by this turn of events and threatened to arrest peasants who were taking matters into their own hands. From February to September retaliation against the Camisards took the form of patrols, the interruption of assemblies, and the execution of Camisards and New Converts.[15]

Meanwhile, skirmishes and punitive expeditions dragged on in the early months of 1703. In March, the united troops of Roland and Cavalier were soundly defeated at Pompignan. The New Converts to Catholicism from Mialet and Saumane, suspected of

---

14. Crété, *Camisards*, 112.
15. Bernat, "Guerre des cévennes," 462–65.

aiding and abetting the Camisards, were deported to Perpignan.[16] On Palm Sunday, April 1, about three hundred Protestants assembled for worship at a mill at Agau near Nîmes. When Montrevel was informed about it, he led a troop of soldiers with orders to break down the door and slit the throats of all present. Irritated by the time-consuming process of the slaughter, he burned down the mill. All perished except for one young woman saved from the flames by the humanity of one soldier. She was hanged the next day and her liberator spared at the last minute through the intercession of nuns.[17] The massacre of Huguenots at illegal assemblies was not new. What made this massacre particularly loathsome was its familial nature, a gathering composed mostly of women and children whose cries from the flames were heard by the bourgeois in the city.[18]

There were reprisals against Catholic villages from Roland and Camisard victories led by Cavalier. Cavalier then suffered defeats near Alès and at Bruyés in April and May as the Camisards waited in vain for intervention by foreign Protestant powers. Amnesty was promised in June 1703 for those who laid down their arms and was interpreted by the Camisards as a sign of weakness. Cévenols, whose homes had been destroyed, swelled the ranks of the Camisards. The combats continued with both resounding victories and stinging defeats for the insurgents.[19]

In September 1703, the king approved Bâville's decision to depopulate the Hautes-Cévennes. All the residents of designated villages were given three days to gather their animals and possessions to move to villages under surveillance. Royal troops under Julien were authorized to burn their houses. Roland and Jouany led reprisals against Catholic villages that in turn led to more retaliation against Protestants. Some Catholics, weary of the inability of the royal troops to master the situation, formed bands of partisans named Cadets de la Croix, Camisards Blancs, or Florentins after

---

16. Carbonnier-Burkard, *Révolte des Camisards*, 70.
17. Ducasse, *Guerre des Camisards*, 120.
18. Crété, *Camisards*, 132–33.
19. Carbonnier-Burkard, *Révolte des Camisards*, 72.

the village of Saint-Florent north of Alès. Bishop Fléchier approved the massacre at the mill of Agau and now supported the Cadets who killed and pillaged people with no connection to the insurrection.[20] Atrocities were committed on both sides. The vengeance of the Camisards was terrifying, and the reprisals were aimed not only at the Camisards but at the Protestant population in general.[21] Even the Bishop of Uzès and General de Paratte admitted that the Cadets de la Croix were as dangerous as the New Converts because they murdered and pillaged both New Converts and Catholics from birth without distinction. Paratte wrote to Chamillart to request that the bishops of Uzès and Alais reside in Paris. He accused them of contributing to the disorder by their presence in the region "through their harshness and injustice."[22]

---

20. Armogathe and Joutard, "Bâville et la guerre," 65.

21. Joutard, *Camisards*, 118–19.

22. Puaux, "Origines, causes et conséquences," 221.

CHAPTER 9

The Devastation of the Cévennes

Montrevel impatiently waited to implement the plan for the devastation of the Cévennes. The plan encompassed the destruction of 466 villages or hamlets, 31 parishes, and the deportation of 13,300 persons.[1] The decree was published in all the cities and villages. Inhabitants of the condemned villages were given three days to gather their animals and some personal effects and travel to twelve villages provisionally spared. The young people left their villages and headed for the woods to join the ranks of the Camisards. Even the Protestant *gentilshommes* who had converted to Catholicism had to leave their châteaux although they were permitted by order of the king to choose the city where they would reside.[2] Priests treated the New Converts harshly and were authorized by their bishops to take up arms against the Camisards. When the order was given to destroy the Cévennes, priests made lists of suspects whose homes were to be destroyed and gave the lists to Julien.[3]

---

1. Ducasse, *Guerre des Camisards*, 129–30.
2. Crété, *Camisards*, 155.
3. Puaux, "Origines, causes et conséquences," 222.

The War of the Camisards (1702–1704)

FAILED ALLIANCE

A former abbot, Antoine de la Bourlie, Marquis of Guiscard, attempted an insurrection in the province of Rouergue with an alliance of Catholics and Protestants to obtain freedom of conscience and lower taxes. From the Cévennes, Cavalier and Roland sent Catinat with some men to rally with Bourlie's men. When everything was in readiness for the uprising, Catinat compromised the endeavor when he attacked and burned down churches and chapels in the region of La Caz, causing the bishop of Castres to seek refuge elsewhere. It became impossible for Bourlie to carry out his plan. By his punitive expedition, Catinat had scuttled the uprising, and Bourlie fled to Switzerland. Some of Catinat's men were arrested and executed. Cavalier's father and brother were arrested, and Cavalier threatened to liberate them with ten thousand men. Montrevel responded by sending 250 dragoons to Ribaute to pillage and level Cavalier's family home. Cavalier led reprisals in the villages of Saturargues and Saint-Cériès with orders to destroy everything and spare no one.[4]

As soon as he received authorization from Versailles, Montrevel left for Saint-Jean-de-Gardonnenque for the final preparations for the devastation of the Cévennes. The king was initially reluctant to order the complete destruction of villages. It was decided to limit the damage to the roofs and floors of houses, a particularly difficult method given the solid stone construction of Cévenol houses. Bâville supported this decision so the homes could be rapidly reconstructed when the situation returned to normal.[5] The workshops of several non-Protestant villages promised to provide hundreds of axes along with shovels and crowbars. Montrevel divided the Cévennes into three sectors. Brigadier Julien was charged with the depopulation and destruction of almost two hundred villages and hamlets in the Pont-de-Montvert region. Marquis de Canillac, an infantry brigadier, was ordered to destroy four communities and several villages in Esperou and Aigoual.

4. Crété, *Camisards*, 156–59.
5. Armogathe and Joutard, "Bâville et la guerre," 66.

Montrevel reserved for himself the vicinity of Barre, where he set up headquarters. Julien left Saint-Jean-de-Gardonnenque with two battalions with a thousand men divided into five groups of two hundred each, with the dismantling of houses to begin on October 1, 1703.[6]

When the troops arrived in the condemned parishes they found only a few women, children, and old men. Everyone else had fled to the forest and caverns, fearful for their lives. Soon Julien understood the enormous task before him and the great difficulty of removing the roofs and floors from houses. Many were built on rock formations, high peaks, and steep slopes in wooded areas or narrow valleys. Due to slow progress, he requested permission from the king's minister to burn the villages. He also recognized that his men were better suited for pillaging and theft than hard work. Montrevel warned that the devastation would take several months to complete. They both believed less and less in the efficiency of the present method, and in October they received permission from the king to burn the villages. There was some apprehension that the new measure would cause those previously undecided to cast their lot with the rebels.[7]

CÉVENNES AFLAME

Julien immediately began to set fires and by October 26 reported the destruction of nine communities. His troops burned down barns and farms before returning to the villages temporarily spared for lodgment, burning the villages upon their departure. From the summits of mountain ridges the Cévenols helplessly watched the flames consume their houses, barns, furnishings, all the memories of a lifetime. In November the villagers in desperation called the Camisard chiefs to their aid. Élie Marion and La Valette contacted Roland and La Rose to join them with their troops, and they resolved to attack the enemy with about six hundred men. However,

6. Crété, *Camisards*, 160.
7. Crété, *Camisards*, 161–62.

The War of the Camisards (1702–1704)

the Spirit told Marion that they would not succeed in preventing the burnings. Roland disagreed that the message came from the Spirit's inspiration and was stopped only when another prophet confirmed the message.[8]

At this time, several Camisard chiefs halted armed resistance to give themselves to the assemblies. Abraham Mazel rarely entered into combat. Salomon Couderc turned his troops over to Jouany and began an itinerant preaching ministry. The Camisards of the mountains appeared to have been seized by lethargy while Cavalier continued in the plains more determined than ever to strike the enemy until freedom of conscience was granted. In October he stood with his troops at the gates of Uzès, kidnapped two sentinels, and launched a challenge for the Marquis de Vergetot to meet him in combat. Cavalier's troops numbered about three hundred men, ninety horsemen, and four women on horses. The opposing forces met near Lussan and both claimed victory. Vergetot reported that he had pursued the Camisards into the woods. Cavalier declared that the enemy had withdrawn in retreat.

While waiting in the woods, Cavalier received a message from Roland to join him to protect the inhabitants of the condemned villages. He found Roland and three thousand Cévenols without shelter gathered at an assembly near Sainte-Croix-Vallée-Française. Roland remained troubled by the revelations of his prophets and was unwilling to mount an operation against Julien. The displaced inhabitants of the villages feared that without help they would be forced to find refuge in closed cities as ordered by Montrevel. Pressured by Cavalier and the villagers, Roland finally decided to act, and the young chiefs agreed to attack Julien from two different directions. The weather was dreadfully cold and rain had made the paths almost impassable. It began to snow and food became scarce. With their provisions exhausted, they had only chestnuts to eat. After hearing that the Florentins and other pillaging bands were persecuting the New Converts in the Vaunage, Cavalier did an about-face and returned to his domain.[9]

8. Ducasse, *Guerre des Camisards*, 133–34; Crété, *Camisards*, 163–64.
9. Crété, *Camisards*, 165–67.

The Devastation of the Cévennes

No province of France had known such devastation since the Hundred Years' War. Death stalked everywhere, not only by Camisards or royal troops but by bands of Catholics that had taken up arms with the support of the clergy. Their objective was less to defend Catholic villages than to pillage, kill, and destroy. The Florentins and Cadets de la Croix roamed the plains to avenge their societal resentment against a more prosperous Protestant community. In authorizing these bands to organize, Montrevel opened the door to abuses. He had hoped to turn them into a disciplined militia, but they were never more than roving pillagers. The raids spread as others were drawn to this lucrative activity. In autumn the bands devastated the region of Bagnols-sur-Cèze. Others were led by the priest of Sainte-Cécile-d'Andorge and killed fifty-two people, including pregnant women at Branoux. Catholic bands from the area of Uzès carried out fruitful expeditions against Saint-Laurens-la-Vernède and Garrigues. Disturbed, Montrevel was forced to recognize that Catholics from six or seven parishes had taken up arms and in cold blood attacked and slaughtered New Converts of their region without regard to sex or age. Montrevel resolved to arrest the pillagers and cracked down on the priest of Sainte-Cécile, arresting him and some leaders. Public order was restored by the end of November, at least temporarily.[10]

Major military confrontations became rare between the Camisards and royal troops, giving place to guerilla warfare. Far from seeking contact with the rebels, Montrevel carefully avoided it and saw the futility of conflict. His earlier courage waned as his superstition grew, and his men lost heart. Throughout the countryside, from Grau-du-Roi to Saintes-Maries, he had burned all the houses or cabins that might shelter the Camisards. He ordered peasants to store their foodstuffs in cities with garrisons in an attempt to starve the Camisards. The province was in a sorry state but the rebels refused to yield. Bâville realized that the Camisards numbered far less than the three thousand men he imagined, their leaders were peasants, and no foreigners were fighting at their

---

10. Crété, *Camisards*, 167–69.

The War of the Camisards (1702–1704)

sides. Yet twenty battalions and twenty regiments of dragoons had not been able to destroy the rebels.

The Camisards maneuvered at will in the plains and forced the royals to exchange prisoners. The militia of Valleraugue kidnapped the wife of Castanet, the famous Blondine. Castanet responded by capturing the wife of the town's consul and threatened the same treatment his wife suffered. The authorities were pressured by the consul and friends of the dame of Valleraugue to make the exchange. As a rule, the Camisards spared the Catholic *gentilshommes* who had not openly opposed them and treated women with deference. Yet murders and reprisals continued on both sides, and the innocent often suffered.[11]

While Julien continued burning villages, amid this cruelty the priest of Mingaud advised the New Converts of his community to remove from their homes anything that might burn to make the work of the destroyers more difficult. Nothing escaped the fury of the king's soldiers. They raped women and girls; massacred the old and infirm, youth and children; and spared only those who consented to the royal decree to live in walled cities and attend Mass. Destruction and death augmented the ranks of the rebels. A rude winter led to a battle for survival as the Camisard leaders struggled to secure food for their troops and for the families who preferred to live together dangerously in the mountains rather than suffer separation in Catholic towns. Since the Huguenots' enemies had sought to starve them by destroying their mills and ovens, they in turn seized the grain and cattle of their adversaries and ambushed the convoys resupplying the garrisons. The Camisard troops and refugees held all things in common as they struggled to survive. Julien returned to Uzès and waited for the next move.[12]

---

11. Crété, *Camisards*, 171–72.
12. Crété, *Camisards*, 176–78.

CHAPTER 10

The Beginning of the End

Despite the destruction and the persecution, Montrevel remained powerless to crush the rebellion. The Camisards roamed freely in the mountains and on the plains. The royal troops stayed in their fortified cities. In December 1703 Cavalier delivered a mortal blow to four regiments commanded by Captain LaBorde and routed the forces of the governor of Saint-Hippolyte. When the year 1704 opened there were rumors about the recall of Montrevel. He still held to the idea of genocide, but the king refused to allow the total destruction of the rebellious region. He undertook a new action called *La visite des paroisses en détail* (Detailed Visit of Parishes), code for arresting fanatics, destroying ovens and mills, confiscating horses, and monitoring shoemakers and blacksmiths. The "visits" were systematically carried out in the dioceses of Uzès, Nîmes, and Alès by Brigadier Planque who boasted of his cruelty in whipping women.[1]

With these measures of suffering inflicted on the Cévenols, Roland and his troops, joined by angry villagers, went on the offensive. Two battalions from Dauphiné were decimated by the Camisards in an ambush on their return from delivering prisoners at La Salle. A considerable amount of booty in arms and ammunition

---

1. Puaux, "Origines, causes et conséquences," 216–17.

THE WAR OF THE CAMISARDS (1702–1704)

was seized along with horses. The dead were stripped of their uniforms and money and Planque burned the bodies to conceal the number killed. Roland and his men celebrated their victory after which they attacked the outskirts of Saint-Hippolyte, burned the church, overturned crosses, and spread terror in the city.[2]

PANIC AND SLAUGHTER

The victory of the Children of God stoked Planque's ferocity. He pillaged the area around La Salle, burned houses in Vallelongues and Roucou, killed several peasants, and whipped women and girls. His soldiers devastated the valley of Saint-Martial and kidnapped all the young people. In one expedition over six hundred New Converts were slaughtered.[3] Montrevel participated personally in this vast operation of cleansing in kidnapping over two hundred people at Nîmes who were taken to the fort. There were few court proceedings or judicial executions since the soldiers often killed their victims where they found them. Over a thousand unarmed New Converts were killed by the king's soldiers or massacred by the Cadets de la Croix between January 1 and August 15, 1704. There were only four official executions during this same period including Marie Mathieu, the *Grande Marie*, for whom Cavalier had deep affection. Cavalier kidnapped the sister of a Florentin leader and sought to exchange her for Marie. Bâville refused the offer and threatened to break Cavalier's father and brother on the wheel if he did not release his hostage. Cavalier returned his prisoner unharmed and the *Grande Marie* was hanged after undergoing torture.[4]

Alarmed and horrified by the atrocities, the New Converts of Nîmes pleaded with Montrevel to intervene. They offered to support the marshal against the Camisards if Montrevel ended the ravages of the Cadets. He responded that the Cadets had the

---

2. Crété, *Camisards*, 180–82.
3. Ducasse, *Guerre des Camisards*, 100.
4. Crété, *Camisards*, 183.

upper hand and the New Converts would be better served if they convinced the Camisards to put down their weapons and surrender. Nevertheless, he published a decree that forbade anyone from being armed in the countryside without his authorization. The decree was not carried out and disorder reigned until Cavalier took the matter in hand to repress the Catholic bands. With a thousand footmen and a hundred horsemen under his command, he carried out reprisals against the villages from where the Cadets originated. Over a hundred Catholics died by their hand, slain as persecutors of the Children of God.[5]

Reinforcements arrived from the Court at the moment when three prophets incited an uprising at the head of a hundred men who burned churches and killed several priests. Once informed, Julien marched on Vivarais, and the repression was terrible. He massacred the inhabitants of the hamlets of Franchassis and Lassange for having sheltered the rebels. The reprisals of Cavalier were equally terrible as he spread terror. The "detailed visits" had brought fresh recruits, and Cavalier reigned as master throughout the plains. He addressed a letter to Marshal Montrevel to explain the reason for his resistance—the freedom of conscience. Montrevel dismissed the letter with disdain and both Cavalier and the Cadets de la Croix continued spreading panic by their violent and retaliatory expeditions. The Cadets stopped voyagers on the road and made them recite the Ave Maria in Latin. Those who did not know the Catholic prayers or recited the Lord's Prayer in French were massacred. Their rage went so far that the abbot of Saint-Gilles protected a domestic servant with his own body to prevent the Cadets from killing her.[6]

CAMISARD VICTORY

The Camisard resistance reached its apogee in early 1704 followed by rapid decline, division, and the surrender of Camisard leaders.

---

5. Crété, *Camisards*, 184–85.
6. Crété, *Camisards*, 186.

The War of the Camisards (1702–1704)

Cavalier multiplied his attacks seizing weapons, intercepting food convoys, killing collaborators, and burning their farms. In March he obtained a stunning victory in open country at Devois-de-Martignargues east of Gardon against one of the best regiments of Languedoc.[7] Montrevel sent La Jonquière with six hundred soldiers after Cavalier, whose men hid in the woods to ambush the royal troops. Cavalier's regular troops took fire from La Jonquière's men who charged with bayonets to finish off the wounded. When they were near the men waiting in ambush, Cavalier and his best marksmen sprang from their hiding places singing the first words of Psalm 51, "Have mercy on me, O God, according to your steadfast love." Over three hundred soldiers and officers paralyzed with fear were killed. Cavalier took the horse of La Jonquière, who had been wounded, and led his men to Vézénobre where they gave thanks to God for a resounding victory.[8]

A soldier escaped and reported the massacre to Montrevel who ordered the Marquis de Lalande to lead troops to the field of battle. Corpses lined the road, and the authorities were shocked that many of the soldiers had been killed with pitchforks. The defeat of La Jonquière frightened the entire province and stunned Versailles. These were some of the king's best troops slaughtered by peasants led by a twenty-two-year-old village baker. The days of Montrevel were numbered in Languedoc. Bâville had addressed a devastating confidential report to Versailles that would have hastened Montrevel's removal even without the defeat at Martignargues. He wrote concerning Montrevel: "I do not believe there is a man in France more incapable in this task. He is like a weather vane controlled for twenty-four hours by whoever turns him. . . . What a great misfortune when one chooses a man unskillful and stupid."[9] The news of Montrevel's imminent departure allowed the Camisards to savor the joys of victory. Cavalier's reputation grew and he was spoken of as a legendary hero. After the battle at Martignargues, he hid the booty in the caves of Euzet and then

---

7. Joutard, *Camisards*, 121.
8. Ducasse, *Guerre des Camisards*, 143.
9. Armogathe and Joutard, "Bâville et la guerre," 58.

rejoined Roland to confer on their next moves. While lodged at Caveirac, Cavalier received false information from a traitor that led him to believe that Montrevel had left for Montpellier with his troops to await his replacement. The Camisard chief believed the field was wide open and planned to strike while the iron was hot and perhaps even attack Nîmes or Sommières.[10]

CAMISARD DEFEAT

Before his departure in disgrace, however, Montrevel wanted to prove himself in battle against Cavalier. He was made aware of Cavalier's troop movements and plans and assembled three thousand troops at Nages near Nîmes on April 17, 1704. Cavalier was drawn into the plains where Montrevel surrounded him and his one thousand men. They refused any quarter and chose to die quickly in battle rather than suffer an agonizing death at the stake. Four hundred were killed and others retreated to the forest in defeat. Nages was a great victory for Montrevel, who left the province with his head held high. In the woods of Euzet, Cavalier and his men tended to their wounds. An informer reported their presence to Lalande, who tried to encircle the rebels. Cavalier fled with most of his men; the wounded left behind were massacred. Lalande went on to pillage Euzet and massacred the inhabitants, except an old woman who at the foot of the gallows promised to reveal the location of Cavalier's stockpiles of weapons and provisions. The king's troops discovered them in the caves of Euzet. This great loss made Cavalier feel vulnerable. He knew replenishment from the impoverished Cévennes population would be difficult. Lalande and his soldiers returned joyfully to Alais with the "ears of their victims on the point of their bayonets."[11]

---

10. Ducasse, *Guerre des Camisards*, 143–44.
11. Ducasse, *Guerre des Camisards*, 145–47.

CHAPTER 11

Negotiations and Surrender

The terrorism of Bâville and the cruelty of Broglie, Montrevel, Planque, and Julien failed to quell the insurrection. Louis XIV sent Marshal de Villars (1653–1734) to Languedoc to replace Montrevel with assurances from the king of limited freedoms and the repudiation of past excesses. Villars was a distinguished soldier and polished diplomat. In his memoirs, he testified that he saw things in the Cévennes that he would never have believed if he had not seen them with his own eyes, entire villages where men and women appeared to be possessed by the devil and young girls trembling and publicly prophesying in the streets. Through discussions with the king and secretary of state, he concluded that the rebels' barbaric actions were due to the relentless, organized persecution they had experienced for the practice of their religion. He considered that further violence would only aggravate the situation and received permission from the king to utilize different methods to pacify the province.[1]

Villars had a wild card in the person of Jacob Rossel, Baron of Aigaliers, a former Protestant who had abjured during the *dragonnades*. Thanks to friends at the Court, Aigaliers presented an ambitious project to those in high places to lead the rebels to lay

---

1. Villars, *Mémoires*, 145–46.

down their arms. The project included the promise of amnesty and the formation of a Camisard regiment commanded by royal officers. The Camisards would conserve their religion and fight for the king at the kingdom's borders. The king would have nothing to do with the project and believed that Aigaliers was a spy. However, the king's minister Chamillart thought otherwise and introduced him to Villars, who showed interest in the project.[2]

APPEASEMENT

Aigaliers and Villars headed to the troubled region and met Brigadier Julien en route. Aigaliers and Julien had a heated argument, and Julien bluntly declared the only way to end the rebellion was to exterminate the rebels and destroy villages under suspicion of aiding and abetting the insurgents. Villars and Aigaliers were welcomed by Bâville, who agreed that extreme means could not end the revolt. Villars laid out a plan to grant amnesty to rebels who surrendered, free detainees arrested on denunciation, and tear down the gallows at Nîmes. He traveled throughout the province, gave hope to people frustrated by years of devastation, and repudiated the excesses of the Catholic clergy.[3] Religious assemblies remained forbidden but people could pray according to their conscience in their homes. The presence of Aigaliers at his side facilitated relations with the New Converts. A week after Villars arrived in Languedoc, thirty-five Camisards surrendered with their arms.[4]

Villars began to understand the situation and the errors of past repressions. It became clear to him that some called themselves Camisards to plunder and murder, others occasionally joined their ranks, and a third group of reasonable people had been pushed to rebel by the cruelty of his predecessor. He hoped this third group would surrender quickly. There was also the realization that many Catholics sought to chase the New Converts from the province

---

2. Crété, *Camisards*, 198–99.
3. Villars, *Mémoires*, 147–48.
4. Crété, *Camisards*, 200.

only to confiscate their property. The actions of the Cadets de la Croix had made the Camisards more determined to resist them. In the meantime, through an intermediary, Bâville contacted Jean Cavalier to probe whether he was open to negotiations. Flattered that a marshal of France wanted to negotiate with him as an equal and not with Roland, Cavalier agreed to send a letter to Villars.[5]

Cavalier had been weakened after the defeat at Nages and the capture of his stores of food and ammunition at Euzet. Lacking resources and confronted by the fresh troops of Villars, Cavalier and his men doubted their ability to continue the struggle. According to Bâville, Cavalier had only three hundred men, with only half of them armed. Some of his men were demoralized and wanted to return to their homes. Villars received Cavalier's letter at Uzès, in which the Camisard chief declared that he would lay down his arms with conditions: the freedom of conscience accorded to Protestants in the kingdom, freedom for prisoners on the king's galleys, and the freedom for him and his men to leave the kingdom. Villars set out with his troops in search of Cavalier and returned empty-handed. He realized the futility of trying to find them and feared getting bogged down like his predecessors. Despite his reassuring speeches, the population did not trust him and refused to provide any information on Cavalier's whereabouts. He was even more pressed by reports of enemy ships along the coast of Languedoc.[6]

CAVALIER'S "BETRAYAL"

After negotiations and the promise of freedom to leave the kingdom, Cavalier signed an armistice and surrendered. Villars sent his aide-de-camp to carry the good news to the king. Concerning the terms of the armistice, Cavalier kept them from other Camisard leaders. He met with Villars and Bâville in Nîmes, and several Camisard chiefs accepted to submit themselves to the mercy of the king, to either leave the kingdom or place themselves in the service

---

5. Ducasse, *Guerre des Camisards*, 154.
6. Crété, *Camisards*, 201–2.

of the king. Cavalier was seduced by Villars's offer to form a regiment of Camisards which he would lead as a colonel. The terms of surrender and demands were sent to Versailles.[7] While waiting for the king's answer, Cavalier and his men went to Calvisson where the other Camisard chiefs would gather. Villars and Cavalier exchanged letters in May and June in which Cavalier expressed his troops' displeasure at learning that "they must leave the first of the month without having seen their relatives and friends freed." Villars responded that "the king would permit the freedom of prisoners" but there had been no promise made concerning the practice of their religion and that the king had the same power as German princes who forbade the practice of the Catholic religion in their realms.[8]

Cavalier met Roland at Durfort, informed him of the negotiations, and exhorted him to surrender. Roland announced he would not go to Calvisson until they received the reply from the Court. People began to gather by the thousands, and assemblies were held on the ruins of the temple. Even priests hurried to Calvisson out of curiosity. Rumors spread that those exiled would return, those imprisoned would be freed, galley slaves would be liberated, the New Converts would be no longer constrained to attend Mass, and those serving under Cavalier in a new regiment would be permitted to have their own ministers. In their enthusiasm, many believed King Louis XIV had been touched by grace and granted full religious freedom. When the king's response came, they learned that he was prepared to free those imprisoned for their faith and allow Reformed believers to leave the kingdom, but he had no intention of having a regiment of Camisards. Cavalier and his men were free to go into exile. None of his other conditions were met. It was out of the question for the king to grant freedom of conscience or the return of exiles. Cavalier finally admitted to other leaders that he received orders to leave and serve the king in Portugal and confessed that he had obtained nothing regarding the freedom of

---

7. Crété, *Camisards*, 210–11.
8. Villars, *Mémoires*, 311–14.

conscience or worship. The people were broken and saw the end of a dream.[9]

EXILES AND EXECUTIONS

After a visit to Versailles where it seems he was not permitted to see the king, Cavalier and one hundred of his men were escorted by the king's soldiers from the province, never to return. The remaining Camisards in the Cévennes considered Cavalier a traitor. After Cavalier's surrender, Roland gathered over a thousand troops to continue the struggle. He received news that allied ships would arrive soon and was promised arms, ammunition, and money. The situation in the Cévennes was chaotic. There was a failed expedition by Protestant allies and Villars restarted military operations. The king was growing impatient, having expected a complete surrender of all the Camisards. Prisons were once again filled with suspects. Aigaliers attempted to negotiate with Roland and wrote to Villars about his meeting with "a seditious, ferocious people, preaching and prophesying." After a long speech by Aigaliers, Roland responded that he and his men had no intention of surrendering. Aigaliers was accused of being a hypocrite, Sadducee, and Pharisee and expressed his wish to Villars that "the false prophets and preachers perish."[10]

Roland continued the struggle after assurances of assistance from the envoy of foreign allies. He was betrayed and killed in August in a château near Uzès.[11] His five companions surrendered and were executed at Nîmes: Jean Maillet, Charles Raspal, Jacques Guérin, Marc Antoine Cousterelle, and François Grimaud, all young men in their twenties. Convinced they were dying for a just cause, they manifested neither weakness nor regrets. As they bravely suffered, Roland's corpse was burned nearby. Bonbonnoux mourned his death and grieved over the surrender of other

---

9. Crété, *Camisards*, 216–17.
10. Villars, *Mémoires*, 316–18.
11. Joutard, *Camisards*, 197; Villars, *Mémoires*, 158–59.

Camisard leaders. The remaining Camisards were further demoralized, and troops led by Ravanel disbanded and escaped to the forest. Their days were marked by dissension, hunger, fear, and despair. Sensing the cause lost, the Camisard leaders surrendered one by one—Castanet, Jouany, Couderc—and they were permitted to leave France for Switzerland.[12] With most of its leaders dead or exiled the war was nearly terminated. Some leaders, however, returned to France and were hunted down. In frustration, Brigadier Planque wrote to Chamillart, "I am seeking by all means through ambushes and manhunts to trap Claris and his companion [Bonbonnoux] who are the last two remaining in this canton."[13]

In exile, Cavalier led a regiment of Huguenot refugees in the service of the Duke of Savoy. He was wounded and defeated at the Battle of Almanza in Spain in 1707, and his regiment was annihilated. It would be his last combat. Although he fought on the side of the English, many Protestants remain proud of his courageous stand against tyranny. They regret that he did not die a hero on the battlefield.[14] His life did not end in violent death like other Camisard leaders. Cavalier found refuge in England and Ireland, married a French refugee, and wrote his memoirs in London. In his memoirs, although he downplayed the role of prophetism during the war, *Le théâtre sacré des Cévennes* (*The Sacred Theater of the Cévennes*), a collection of testimonies from Abraham Mazel and other Camisard prophets, provides evidence of consulting prophets and prophetesses during the war.[15] Cavalier ended his military career as major general and governor of the Isle of Jersey where he died in May 1740. Even in exile, he never forgot his native Cévennes or the times of trouble and was associated with repeated attempts to infiltrate France's borders.[16]

Villars was replaced by Marshal Berwick, and the remaining Camisards held out hope for foreign intervention. Castanet, leader

---

12. Crété, *Camisards*, 243–44; Villars, *Mémoires*, 162–63.
13. Bonbonnoux, *Mémoires*, 4.
14. Poujol, "Jean Cavalier," 93–94.
15. Bost, "Prophètes des Cévennes," 408–9.
16. Crété, *Camisards*, 275–76.

The War of the Camisards (1702–1704)

of the Mont Aigoual region, was captured and died on the rack before ten thousand spectators at Montpellier. To the two priests exhorting him to recant he cried, "Withdraw from me, grasshoppers from the pit of the abyss."[17] One final attempt at revolt in the spring of 1705 was a conspiracy to kidnap Marshal Berwick and Bâville to make Bâville pay for his cruelty and deliver Berwick to an English navy ship.[18] The bishops of Nîmes and Montpellier would be taken hostage and a port secured for the disembarkation of the English at Sète or Aigues-Mortes. Ravanel and Catinat remained at Nîmes for the final preparations and Bonbonnoux and Claris went to Montpellier. The plot was discovered and over two hundred conspirators perished.

A wave of terror broke over Montpellier and Nîmes that even shocked Catholics. Anyone suspected of aiding the conspiracy was executed, with or without evidence, millers, farmers, and especially merchants from Nîmes. Their executioners were struck by the fearlessness of the condemned who endured torture with fortitude. Others were sent to the galleys or exiled. Bonbonnoux and Claris refused to surrender or abandon the Cévennes.[19] They escaped from Montpellier but Catinat and Ravanel were captured. The judges discussed the means of execution, whether drawn by horses or burned alive. The majority voted for the fire to prolong their agony. They were executed at Nîmes, dressed in shirts covered with sulfur, and burned at the stake, singing Psalm 51, asking God to forgive all their sins.[20]

Berwick then returned to the more humane methods of his predecessor and offered amnesty to those who surrendered. La Rose and Élie Marion continued their futile resistance, finally surrendered, and were permitted to leave the kingdom. Abraham Mazel joined them on the road of exile to Geneva after escaping from the Tower of Constance at Aigues-Mortes with sixteen of his companions, three of whom were captured and eight surrendered.

17. Ducasse, *Guerre des Camisards*,185–86.
18. Joutard, *Camisards*, 202.
19. Ducasse, *Guerre des Camisards*, 193–95.
20. Crété, *Camisards*, 258–59.

Mazel, like most others with him, had never seen a pastor or worshiped in a temple. They expected a hero's welcome and wanted to continue the struggle but were told all military operations had been suspended. The pastors and consistories that had never approved of the rebellion or conspiracies put the prophets in their place. Moving on to London, the prophets became known as the "French Prophets," announced the destruction of the city by fire and sulfur, and were declared fakes by the churches.[21] Far from the devastation of Languedoc with its gallows, combats, massacres, and persecution, the exploits of the Camisards were incomprehensible and dubious. The prophets were chased from French churches in London and escaped to another town. They were told by the Spirit to return to London and were accused of being Jesuit imposters. Three of the Camisard prophets were arrested, fined, and placed in stocks in December 1707. Jean Cavalier traveled to London and without difficulty convinced Mazel to return to France accompanied by Daniel Guy and Antoine Dupont.[22]

Mazel arrived in the Cévennes and addressed a letter to the clergy demanding the return of the privileges of the Edict of Nantes. He and sixty peasants resisted for one year against the royal troops before Mazel's betrayal and death on October 7, 1710. His companions were hanged or put to death on the rack. Mazel's head was hung for three days at Vernoux, then burned with the ashes thrown to the wind. Claris, wounded and captured at the time of Mazel's death, was broken on the wheel. The Duke of Roquelaure described Claris's execution in a letter to Chamillart: "Claris was judged yesterday by M. Bâsville and the tribune of this city and condemned to the penalties he deserved . . . he died with all the ferocity and obstinacy of a scoundrel hardened by his crime since long ago."[23] These deaths marked the tragic and heroic end of the Camisards.[24]

---

21. Chabrol, "Diffusion et filiations," 147–48.
22. Crété, *Camisards*, 264–67.
23. Bonbonnoux, *Mémoires*, 10.
24. Ducasse, *Guerre des Camisards*, 220–21.

CHAPTER 12

Postscript to War

French Protestants had learned that between God and the king, they could not choose God. They had to choose the God of the king. Among the European powers, France remained the most intolerant in religious matters. The progress of reason was slow to advance in the minds of religious leaders and the common people. "The time [for reason] had not yet arrived."[1] Several years after the War of the Camisards, Louis XIV issued a declaration in March 1715 stating that all subjects of the king were also subjects of the Catholic Church. The falsehood persisted that there were no longer any Reformed believers in France. Anyone who declared that he or she wanted to live and die in the So-Called Reformed Religion, whether they recanted or not, was considered Catholic and the refusal of the sacraments exposed them to punishment. They were not allowed to leave France and, since they remained in France and the practice of their religion was abolished, they were Catholics.[2]

---

1. Voltaire, *Siècle de Louis XIV*, 426.
2. Félice, *Histoire des Protestants*, 424–25.

ANTOINE COURT

The hostility of the Catholic Church to New Converts and the shame of those who made insincere conversions led to the slow reestablishment of Reformed churches. Prophets and prophetesses did not completely disappear, and after 1710 they were at times the only ones to maintain Protestant piety. The state of Reformed churches was lamentable and necessitated a response. Antoine Court (1696–1760) became the primary influencer in reestablishing Reformed churches on a solid doctrinal foundation.[3] From humble beginnings, Antoine Court became known for remarkable exploits of faith during a long and sorrowful period in French history. Court was born in Villeneuve-de-Berg in Vivarais and was baptized in the Catholic faith as required by law. He accompanied his mother to the illegal assemblies of the Church of the Desert where prophetesses had replaced exiled pastors. In 1713 prophets ordered him to write threatening letters to church and government leaders.[4] Following the non-realization of prophecies, he broke with the movement of prophetism, rejected violence previously associated with the Camisards, and fought to reverse the consequences of the Revocation of the Edict of Nantes. In defiance of the king's decree, Court, accompanied by the former Camisard Bonbonnoux, gathered a small group of believers to lay new foundations for Reformed churches in France in rejecting violence and prophetism. The struggle was intense since Court had grown up in the milieu of the prophetesses of Vivarais, whom his mother venerated.[5]

NON-VIOLENT RESISTANCE

The concern for faithfulness to gospel teaching inspired peaceful resistance. The drift of prophetism, far removed from a biblical foundation, had placed the doctrinal survival of the Reformed

3. Bost, "Prophètes des Cévennes," 411.
4. Joutard, *Camisards*, 217.
5. Crété, *Camisards*, 273.

The War of the Camisards (1702–1704)

faith in danger.[6] In addition, the Reformed community was unable to sustain new uprisings. In abandoning violence, the Church of the Desert entered a new phase in 1715 under the leadership of Court. He considered four conditions necessary for the reorganization of Reformed churches: regular public gatherings, the disavowal of the disorder caused by those claiming the Holy Spirit's inspiration, the establishment of church order through consistories and synods, and rigorous training for pastors. The execution of this plan was accompanied by great difficulties. Yet on August 21, 1715, only ten days before the death of Louis XIV, the most powerful monarch of Europe, Court organized the first synod of the Church of the Desert at Montèzes to replant the church that Louis XIV had sought to abolish.[7]

Protestant believers continued to meet clandestinely and were arrested and condemned for worshiping illegally in the decades to follow. The years 1715 to 1760 became known as the "heroic period" of the Church of the Desert when Protestant gatherings were forbidden and those arrested were severely punished. The assemblies took place during the day when the danger subsided, and at night when the risks increased. Time and place were revealed only a few hours before the meeting by trusted messengers. Unarmed sentinels stood guard in high places to signal the approach of soldiers. Rarely did a pastor spend more than a few days in one place. Wandering from place to place, often disguised and at times using fictitious names, they hid as if they were lawbreakers. Worship in the wilderness had the same simplicity as in times of freedom: liturgical prayers, singing psalms, preaching, and the Lord's Supper. There was always the sentiment of danger as they stood and worshiped in the presence of their sovereign Lord.[8]

Louis XIV's death sparked great hope among the Huguenots, both in the kingdom and in exile, for the reestablishment of the Edict of Nantes. Their hope did not long survive. Of the six signatories of church regulations adopted at the synod, four

6. Joutard, *Camisards*, 222.
7. Stéphan, *Épopée huguenote*, 275.
8. Félice, *Histoire des Protestants*, 431–32.

were executed. After the arrest of a young preacher, Étienne Arnaud, Court opposed a project to liberate him forcibly. Arnaud was put to death by hanging at Alès in the presence of a large crowd on January 22, 1718. His death had a profound impact on Protestants beyond the Cévennes region, and he was honored as a martyr for the cause of freedom. Two years later, in the region of Nîmes, another assembly was called with Court and other leaders of the Church of the Desert. The king's troops intervened, and Court escaped, but fifty others were arrested. As an example to others, twenty men were initially condemned as galley slaves for life before the sentence was commuted to deportation. They were transported through France to La Rochelle and exiled to England.[9] On several occasions, Court and his companions prevented new outbreaks of violence with great difficulty. The sons and grandsons of Camisards never completely repudiated their ancestors and were prepared to adopt the same methods of resistance.

LOUIS XV

Louis XV (1710–74), also known as Louis the Beloved, reaffirmed the Edict of Revocation with the Declaration of 1724 proclaiming France a Catholic nation. Protestants who had converted to Catholicism and then returned to Protestantism were considered "relapsed" and were subject to harsh penalties. The declaration contained eighteen articles. They included condemnation for life to the galleys for men and imprisonment for life for women, with confiscation of possessions for participation at non-Catholic religious gatherings. Pastors again faced the death penalty by hanging rather than at the stake or broken on the wheel as in the past. Parents were ordered to have their infants baptized by the parish priest and children were required to follow Catholic catechism until the age of fourteen. There was no legitimate marriage apart from its celebration in the Catholic Church and certificates of

---

9. Joutard, "Antoine Court," 75–76.

The War of the Camisards (1702–1704)

catholicity were required for employment and higher education.[10] During the reign of Louis XV, there were ministers hanged on the Esplanade of Montpellier, and François Roquette was executed in Toulouse in 1762. The three Grenier brothers attempted to free him and were decapitated. Marie Durand was imprisoned from 1730 to 1768 in the Tower of Constance at Aigues-Mortes. The last two galley prisoners were freed in 1775.[11]

Although the royal decree of 1724 was applied sporadically and inconsistently throughout the kingdom, there was great consternation among Protestants. Submission was unthinkable, further emigration might announce the end of French Protestantism, and armed revolt would annul the decision ten years earlier when Protestants had chosen a strategy of non-violence. Their response had two parts. On one hand, they planned to organize peaceful public gatherings to demonstrate to the authorities that French Protestants still existed in the kingdom. The assemblies would disperse at the announcement of the arrival of troops. On the other hand, they would refuse to participate in Catholic ceremonies, particularly baptism, marriage, and extreme unction. It fell to Antoine Court at a synod in 1725 to convince Protestants of the wisdom of these actions. He reminded his listeners of Louis XIV's attempt to destroy Protestantism and how through the years God had raised up leaders to sustain his people.[12]

In his writings, Court addressed what he believed was the greatest problem in reorganizing Reformed churches—the War of the Camisards. He emphasized a distinction between the present assemblies of the Church of the Desert organized by pastors and past assemblies characterized by prophecies and violence. In his rejection of self-proclaimed prophets and prophetesses, his goal was the return of churches to the pre-Revocation pastoral model of leadership, to refrain from violence, and to submit to political authority. This change of strategy had the intention of winning the battle of public opinion in France and among those in exile.

10. Félice, *Histoire des Protestants*, 433–35.
11. Ducasse, *Guerre des Camisards*, 230.
12. Garrisson, *Histoire des Protestants*, 199.

Postscript to War

Although Court separated from those who claimed prophetic inspiration, he remained surrounded by many who had participated in the War of the Camisards. For those who had experienced systematic persecution, conversion to non-violent resistance was difficult to accept. In his book, *History of the Troubles of the Cévennes*, Court showed how intolerance and the dearth of spiritual leadership contributed to the impossibility of controlling processes that led to violence instigated by the prophetic utterances of Camisard leaders. He insisted that the situation following the rebellion influenced his strategy of non-violence, which was more consistent with evangelical principles. Yet to his opponents, Court remained a prisoner of a mindset that accorded undeserved reverence to the monarchy.[13]

In 1729, Court left France permanently to find refuge at Lausanne. There he founded a seminary in 1730, which he directed until his death in 1760. Through his writings, he continued defending Protestants from accusations of treason against the monarchy.[14] In his later writings, he sought to reconcile the early Camisard period of violence with the non-violent reorganized Church of the Desert under his leadership. It seems, however, that he could not admit that the insurrection of the Camisards facilitated the passage to non-violence and that the fear of a new uprising held the authorities in check. His collection of over one hundred volumes of testimonies and letters from galley slaves and exiles constitutes the greatest and most varied source of the history of the Church of the Desert.[15]

Antoine Court found himself confronted by questions beyond his time that resonate in the twenty-first century. How should Christians respond to state-sanctioned persecution? Do Christians ever have the right to take up arms against an established government or another religion? What sustains people in times of persecution and enables them to accept imprisonment or death rather than renounce their faith? Even if Court did not always have

---

13. Joutard, "Antoine Court," 76.
14. Bost, *Histoire des Protestants*, 168.
15. Joutard, "Antoine Court," 77–78.

THE WAR OF THE CAMISARDS (1702–1704)

the right response, he asked the right questions for the benefit of a minority defending their faith, values, and culture. Although he adopted a strategy of non-violence and submission to political authority, his objective remained the same as the Camisards'—obtain the freedom of conscience, the freedom to be born, to live, and to die outside a state religion. His writings and position on relations between religion and state and the fear of a new Camisard uprising undoubtedly contributed to the religious tolerance that eventually gained ground in Languedoc and throughout France. He did not live to see Protestants granted tolerance in 1787 under Louis XVI (1754–93) or religious freedom in 1789 with the arrival of the French Revolution.

CHAPTER 13

Conclusion

At the dawn of the French Revolution in December 1789, the Constituent Assembly granted full civil and political rights to Protestants and established the principle of the freedom of religion that would permit future progress.[1] The Declaration of the Rights of Man and of the Citizen announced a new era of religious tolerance and permitted access to civilian and military positions for non-Catholics: According to Article 10, "No one may be disturbed on account of his opinions, even religious ones, as long as the manifestation of such opinions does not interfere with the established Law and Order." For a time, this statement remained an ideal yet served as a reference point and foundation for future changes.[2] After three centuries of epic resistance and unimaginable suffering, Protestants finally achieved the longing of their hearts—freedom of conscience.

NAPOLEON BONAPARTE

The Revolution was interrupted by the rise to power of Napoleon Bonaparte in 1799 to limit the Revolution's chaotic aspects and

---

1. Crété, *Camisards*, 279–80.
2. Garrisson, *Histoire des Protestants*, 232.

impose new ideals after his impressive conquests. An alliance with the Catholic Church became a political necessity since many French were still attached to their traditional religion. Napoleon desired to establish religious peace and Pope Pius VII wanted to restore the unity of the Church. The Catholic Church's prestige was restored under the terms of the Concordat with Rome in 1801. The Organic Articles were added in 1802 providing state recognition of the Reformed and Lutheran confessions alongside the Catholic Church. Napoleon refused the pope's request that Catholicism be declared the state religion. According to the Concordat's preamble, Catholicism remained the religion of "the majority of French citizens."[3] The majority of Protestant pastors welcomed official recognition. They sacrificed a part of their religious independence and gained salaries from the State. After over a century of struggle following the Revocation of the Edict of Nantes in 1685, and despite government control of religious matters, it was not surprising that many Protestants enthusiastically greeted the Concordat and Organic Articles imposed by Napoleon. Protestants were given access to most public positions and many were won over to the natural religion of the philosophers and the Cult of the Supreme Being. They saw in theocratic deism the end of confessional conflict and the sentiment of belonging to a sect.[4]

In the early 1800s, a religious awakening (*Réveil*) in French Reformed churches took place in Geneva and France. While the façade of religion remained, many churches had drifted from their Reformation moorings. The religion of Calvin had progressed from the austerity, moral vigilance, and dogmatism of the first Calvinists to a natural religion, a religion of common sense, a religion deeply in need of a spiritual awakening.[5]

---

3. Encrevé, *Protestants et la vie*, 74.
4. Garrisson, *Histoire des Protestants*, 235.
5. Maury, *Réveil religieux*, 11–12.

CONCLUSION

END OF THE BOURBON DYNASTY

Upon his arrival on the throne in 1814, Louis XVIII (1755–1824) made it known that he did not want to be king of a divided France. The Charter of 1814 established a constitutional monarchy, guaranteed civil liberties and religious toleration, and reestablished Catholicism as the state religion. Charles X (1757–1836) took the throne in 1824, incarnated the sentiment of the *Ancien Régime*,[6] and enacted measures to increase the power of the Catholic Church for national stability. Bishops were given authority in religious education in secondary schools, and primary school teachers required a teaching certificate from a bishop. The July Revolution in 1830 forced Charles's abdication, and the Chamber of Deputies called Louis-Philippe, Duke of Orléans, as king (1773–1850), the last king of the Bourbon dynasty. During his reign, Catholicism was no longer the state religion and returned to the position of the Concordat as the religion of most French citizens. Louis-Napoleon Bonaparte (1808–73), a nephew of Napoleon Bonaparte, was elected France's first president in 1848 and declared himself emperor of the Second Empire in 1852. In 1859 Protestants celebrated the Jubilee of the first national synod of 1559. They recalled 1559, when Protestants were burned at the stake, the year 1629, when the Edict of Nantes was changed into an Edict of Grace by Cardinal Richelieu before its Revocation in 1685, and the year 1759, when Protestants were semi-tolerated without any legal rights and still subject to persecution.

THIRD REPUBLIC

The end of the Second Empire was followed by the Third Republic (1870–1940) which witnessed a Protestant influence that had been minimal until this time. In the last decades of the nineteenth century, there was an ongoing struggle between anticlerical, republican forces, loyal to the principles of the 1789 Revolution, and

---

6. The *Ancien Régime* describes the political, economic, and social organization of the monarchy in France before 1789 (*Petit Robert*, 2165).

The War of the Camisards (1702–1704)

monarchists who sought the return of the union of the church and monarchy. Protestants sided largely with defenders of the Revolution and opposed any return to an alliance of religious and political powers dominated by the Catholic Church. Political events, including the Dreyfus Affair and the increased influence of the Catholic Church, favored the rise of a movement toward a secular form of government free from religious entanglements and royalist aspirations. The Concordat and Organic Articles survived for one hundred years to navigate the conflicts between religion and state in France before their abrogation by France's Law of Separation of Church and State in 1905. The law ended the 1801 Concordat between Napoleon and the Vatican, disestablished the Catholic Church, and declared state neutrality in religious matters.

Historians remain divided in their assessment of the War of the Camisards. For some, the Camisards were murderous, bloodthirsty scoundrels from the dregs of society who were ignorant of the codes of warfare. Attempts to exterminate them were justified. For others, they were heroes, and their exploits are legendary and worthy of celebration. Attempts to exterminate them failed. The simple truth is that despite everything for which they might be reproached, the Camisards, whose temples had been destroyed, whose villages were burned to the ground, whose loved ones had been massacred, were defending their faith. In any case, the Camisards had not fought in vain. With their hunting rifles, pitchforks, pruning hooks, and sickles, their persecutors felt what a violated religious conscience pushed to its limits was capable of doing. Their wrath overflowed in violent retaliation. From afar, it is easy to judge them for their excesses. But they were not charlatans, scoundrels, blasphemers, or the devil's henchmen, according to the terms used of them at the time. They fought for a just cause against religious oppression using questionable methods. All they requested was the freedom of conscience to worship God. At any time Louis XIV could have restored the Edict of Nantes and ended the war.

What might we learn from this war for our time in history and the current situation? We are far removed from the 1700s in

Conclusion

France when royal troops traveled for days to a far-flung province to quell a rebellion, when guerilla warfare in rugged terrain gave an advantage to the insurgents, and when arms used inflicted fewer mass casualties. In most places today any armed uprisings would be short-lived and futile. Yet, we might ask ourselves some questions. After having exhausted all legal recourse, how should citizens respond to government-sponsored persecution and the denial of religious freedom? Do people ever have the right to rise up against oppressive governments to defend God-given rights? If the government comes for your children and its agents abuse members of your family, do you have the right to self-defense? We have the benefit of hindsight and three hundred years of theological reflection, which they lacked, so our answers might differ from those of Christians in the early 1700s. Although these questions are theoretical for most Westerners, at least for now, Christians elsewhere suffer and die as martyrs as Christians have done throughout the centuries following the example of the early church.[7]

The War of the Camisards was born from persecution and showed an astonished world that Protestantism in France could not be eradicated through persecution. When the state killed the preachers, it created the prophets. When it killed the prophets, it created the Camisards. Who knows if Protestantism would have survived in France without their intervention or disappeared as its enemies had hoped? French historians Henri Bosc, Martin Pin, and Charles Bost are convinced that the War of the Camisards was the salvation of Protestantism.[8] The war had a double effect—Protestants were reassured of their capacity to resist, and the royal court was apprehensive about its strategy of oppression. From their little corner of southern France, their combat for the freedom of conscience was echoed by eighteenth-century philosophers and contributed to the freedom of religion recognized today as a universal right. The War of the Camisards, the devastation of

---

7. "Open Doors estimates the number of Christians killed for faith-related reasons worldwide was 5,621 in 2023, 5,898 in 2022, and 4,761 in 2021." Robinson and Loft, "Religious Persecution," para. 3.

8. Bosc and Allier, "Guerre des Camisards," 353–54.

The War of the Camisards (1702–1704)

the Cévennes, the atrocities committed in the name of religion, and the damage to the image of France serve as warnings for governments to tread lightly in religious matters and for Christians to weigh carefully how to respond to government repression. We remember the War of the Camisards, the sufferings experienced and the sufferings inflicted "not only out of respect for the victims but also so that similar tragedies never take place again."[9]

---

9. Crété, "Guerre des Camisards," 129.

Chronology

1515–47	Reign of Francis I
1517	Luther's Ninety-Five Theses
1521	Jacques Lefèvre at Meaux
1533	Marguerite of Navarre and Calvin in Nérac
1534	Affaire of the Placards
1536	Calvin's *Institutes of the Christian Religion* in Latin
1541	Calvin's *Institutes of the Christian Religion* in French
1545–63	Council of Trent, Counter-Reformation
1559	First National Synod of Reformed churches
	Confession of Faith
	Definitive edition of *Institutes of the Christian Religion* in Latin
	Death of Henry II
1560	Conspiracy of Amboise
	Michel de L'Hospital appointed chancellor
1561	Colloquy of Poissy

Chronology

1562	Edict of January (Catherine de' Medici)
	Massacre of Huguenots at Vassy
1562–98	Wars of Religion
1563	Edict of Amboise
1568	Peace of Longjumeau
1570	Peace of Saint-Germain-en-Laye
1572	Marriage of Henry of Navarre and Marguerite de Valois
	Saint Bartholomew's Day Massacre
1576	Edict of Beaulieu
1585	Henry III outlaws Reformed religion
	Henry of Navarre excommunicated
1589	Assassination of Henry III
1593	Conversion of Henry of Navarre to Catholicism
1594	Coronation of Henry IV at Chartres
1598	Edict of Nantes ends eighth War of Religion
1610	Assassination of Henry IV
1628	Fall of La Rochelle (Louis XIII and Cardinal Richelieu)
1629	Peace of Alès (Edict of Grace)
1643	Louis XIV begins reign
1659	Last Reformed synod at Loudun
1681	*Dragonnades* unleashed to force Protestant conversions to Catholicism
1683	Claude Brousson's non-violent resistance

Chronology

1685	Revocation of the Edict of Nantes
	Bâville sent to govern Languedoc
1685–1715	Massive emigration
1686	First appearance of *prédicants* (preachers) in the Cévennes
1688	Prophetic movement in Vivarais (Isabeau Vincent)
1689	Return from exile of Claude Brousson and François Vivent
1692	Death of Vivent
1697	Treaty of Ryswick
1698	Execution of Brousson
1699	Execution or exile of last *prédicants*
1700	Prophetism in the Cévennes
1702–13	War of Spanish Succession
1702–4	War of the Camisards
1702	Assassination of Abbot du Chaila
	Pierre Séguier (Esprit) burned at the stake
	First major battle at Champdomergue
	Death of Camisard leader Gédéon Laporte
1703	Camisards defeat Broglie and kill Captain Poul
	Montrevel replaces Broglie
	Castanet massacres population of Fraissinet-de-Fourques
	Montrevel massacres assembly at the mill of Agau
	Defeat of Camisards at Pompignan

Chronology

	Failed attempt to extend insurrection in Rouergue
	Formation of Catholic militias
	Devastation of the Cévennes
1704	Detailed Visit of Parishes
	Cavalier's victory at Devois-de-Martignargues
	Villars replaces Montrevel
	Marie Mathieu executed
	Cavalier's supplies discovered in caves of Euzet
	Negotiations between Cavalier and Villars
	Surrender and exile of Jean Cavalier
	Death of Roland
1705	Abraham Mazel arrested and imprisoned in the Tower of Constance
	Berwick replaces Villars
	Marie *la Blondine* imprisoned in Tower of Constance
	Plot to capture Bâville and Berwick
	Execution of Castanet at Montpellier
	Execution of Catinat (Abdias Maurel) and Ravanel at Nîmes
	Abraham Mazel escapes from the Tower of Constance
1706	Cavalier defeated at Almanza
1707	Prophets in London
1709	Abraham Mazel returns to France from exile

Chronology

1710	Execution of Abraham Mazel
1715	Death of Louis XIV
1715	Antoine Court and Synod at Montèzes
1718	Execution of *prédicant* Étienne Arnaud
1724	Louis XV reaffirms Edict of Revocation
1729	Antoine Court leaves France for Lausanne
1730	Antoine Court founds seminary in Lausanne
1740	Death of Cavalier in exile
1755	Death of Bonbonnoux in Lausanne
1762	Last Reformed pastor executed
1768	Last prisoners liberated from Tower of Constance
1775	Last two prisoners released from king's galleys
1787	Edict of Toleration (Louis XVI)
1789	French Revolution
1799	Napoleon's rise to power
1801	Concordat with Rome
1802	Organic Articles
1814	Charter of Louis XVIII
1824	Charles X
1830	July Revolution
	Louis-Philippe, Duke of Orléans
1848	Louis-Napoleon elected France's first president
1852	Louis-Napoleon declares himself emperor

Chronology

1859	Protestants celebrate Jubilee of First National Synod of 1559
1870	Third Republic
1905	Law of Separation of Church and State

From the Same Author

Crossing Cultures: Preparing Strangers for Ministry in Strange Places. Eugene, OR: Wipf & Stock, 2019.

"France's Long March from State Religion to Secular State." In *The Palgrave Handbook of Religion and State Volume II: Global Perspectives*, edited by Shannon Holzer, 127–50. Cham, Switz.: Palgrave-Macmillan, 2023.

The French Huguenots and Wars of Religion: Three Centuries of Violence for Freedom of Conscience. Eugene, OR: Wipf & Stock, 2021.

French Protestantism's Struggle for Survival and Legitimacy, 1517–1905. Eugene, OR: Wipf & Stock, 2023.

God's Unchanging Word in an Ever-Changing World: Messages of Hope for Weary Christians. Eugene, OR: Wipf & Stock, 2022.

Missiological Reflections on Life and Mission. Eugene, OR: Wipf & Stock, 2022.

Rise of French Laïcité: French Secularism from the Reformation to the Twenty-First Century. Eugene, OR: Pickwick, 2020.

Urban Church Planting: Journey into a World of Depravity, Density, and Diversity. Eugene, OR: Resource Publications, 2019.

Bibliography

Armogathe, Jean-Robert, and Philippe Joutard. "Bâville et la consultation des évêques en 1698." *Revue d'histoire et de philosophie religieuses* 52.5 (1972) 157–84. https://www.persee.fr/doc/rhpr_0035-2403_1972_num_52_2_4097.

———. "Bâville et la guerre des camisards." *Revue d'Histoire Moderne et Contemporaine* 19.1 (1972) 45–72. https://www.persee.fr/doc/rhmc_0048-8003_1972_num_19_1_2183.

Babelon, Jean-Pierre. *Henri IV*. Paris: Fayard, 1982.

———. "Henri IV et la Réforme." *Bulletin de la Société de l'Histoire du Protestantisme Français* 156 (Oct.–Dec. 2010) 595–606. http://www.jstor.org/stable/24310105.

Bâville, Nicolas de Lamoignon de. *Mémoires pour servir à l'histoire de Languedoc*. Amsterdam: Pierre Boyer, 1734. https://tinyurl.com/BavilleMemoires.

Bayrou, François. *Henri IV*. Paris: Éditions Flammarion, 1998.

Benedict, Philip, and Nicolas Fornerod. "Les 2,150 'églises' réformées de France de 1561–1562." *Revue Historique* 651 (July 2009) 529–30. https://www.jstor.org/stable/40958448.

Bernat, Chrystel. "La guerre des cévennes: Un conflit trilatéral?" *Bulletin de la Société de l'Histoire du Protestantisme Français* 148 (July–Sept. 2002) 461–507. http://www.jstor.org/stable/43691735.

Bèze, Theodore de. *Confession de la foy chrestienne*. Geneva: Jacques du Pan, 1563. https://tinyurl.com/BezaConfession.

Birnstiel, Eckart. "La conversion des protestants sous le régime de l'Édit de Nantes (1598–1685)." In *Religions, pouvoir et violence*, edited by Patrick Cabanel and Michel Bertrand, 93–113. Toulouse: Presses universitaires du Midi, 2004.

Bonbonnoux, Jacques. *Mémoires de Bonbonnoux. Chef Camisard et Pasteur du Désert*. Cévennes: J. Vielles, 1883. https://tinyurl.com/MemBonbon.

Bosc, Henri. *La guerre des Cévennes, 1702–1710*. Montpellier: Presses du Languedoc, 1993.

BIBLIOGRAPHY

Bosc, Henri, and Jacques Allier. "La Guerre des Camisards: Son caractère. Ses conséquences." *Bulletin de la Société de l'Histoire du Protestantisme Français* 119 (July–Sept. 1973) 335–55. http://www.jstor.org/stable/24294401.

Bost, Charles. *Histoire des Protestants de France*. 9th ed. Carrières-sous-Poissy, FR: Éditions La Cause, 1996.

———. *Les Prédicants Protestants des Cévennes et du Bas-Languedoc, 1684–1700*. Paris: Honoré Champion, 1912. https://archive.org/details/lesprdicantspro1bost.

———. "Les 'Prophètes des Cévennes' au XVIIIe siècle." *Revue d'histoire et de philosophie religieuses* 5.5 (Sept.–Oct. 1925) 401–30. https://www.persee.fr/doc/rhpr_0035-2403_1925_num_5_5_2547.

Bost, Hubert. Review of *Histoire du fanatisme renouvelé*, by Jean-Baptiste L'Ouvreleul. *Études théologiques et religieuses* 77.3 (2002) 443. https://www.persee.fr/doc/ether_0014-2239_2002_num_77_3_4855_t1_0443_0000_3.

Brachet, Auguste. *An Etymological Dictionary of the French Language*. Translated by G. W. Kitchin. Oxford: Clarendon, 1882. https://tinyurl.com/BrachetDictionary.

Brousson, Claude. *Relation Sommaire des Merveilles que Dieu fait en France*. Mountain View, CA: Éditions Ionas, 2016. https://archive.org/details/1694BroussonRelationSommairetireAPart.

Brueys, David-Augustin de. *Histoire du fanatisme de Nostre Temps*. Montpellier: Jean Martel, 1709. https://gallica.bnf.fr/ark:/12148/bpt6k1040174x.

Cabanel, Patrick, and Philippe Joutard, eds. *Les camisards et leur mémoire, 1702–2002*. Montpellier: Presses du Languedoc, 2002.

Calvin, John. *L'Institution chrétienne (IV)*. 1555. Reprint. Chicago: Éditions Kerygma, 1978.

Carbonnier-Burkard, Marianne. *La révolte des Camisards*. Rennes: Éditions Ouest-France, 2012.

Caunège, Guy. *Les Camisards*. Villeurbanne, FR: Éditions Golias, 1999.

Cavalier, Jean. *Mémoires sur la guerre des Camisards*. Paris: Payot, 2006.

Cazenove, A. de. "Un portrait de Bâville." *Bulletin de la Société de l'Histoire du Protestantisme Français* 54 (Mar.–June 1905) 220–27. https://www.jstor.org/stable/24288164.

Chabrol, Jean-Paul. "Diffusion et filiations dans l'espace protestant: le prophétisme 'cévenol' et le monde au XVIIIe siècle." *Diasporas. Histoire et sociétés* 5 (2004) 146–56. https://www.persee.fr/doc/diasp_1637-5823_2004_num_5_1_965.

———. *Les Camisards et la conquête de la liberté de conscience*. Nîmes: Éditions Alcide, 2019.

———. "Le prophétisme cévenol de 1685 à 1702." *Bulletin de la Société de l'Histoire du Protestantisme Français* 148 (Jan.–Mar. 2002) 211–16. http://www.jstor.org/stable/43691639.

Coquerel, Charles. *Histoire des églises du désert chez les protestants de France, depuis la fin du règne de Louis XIV jusqu'à la révolution française*. Paris:

BIBLIOGRAPHY

Librairie Cherbuliez, 1841. https://archive.org/details/histoiredesgliso ocoqugoog.

Cottret, Bernard. *Historie de la Réforme Protestante, XVIe-XVIIIe siècle*. Paris: Perrin, 2010.

Court, Antoine. *Histoire des troubles des Cévennes ou de la guerre des camisards sous le règne de Louis le Grand*. Montpellier: Presses du Languedoc, 2002.

Crété, Liliane. *Les Camisards*. Paris: Éditions Perrin, 2007.

———. "La guerre des Camisards et ses héros." *Bulletin de la Société de l'Histoire du Protestantisme Français* 151 (Jan.–Mar. 2005) 129–33. https://www.jstor.org/stable/24308886.

Crouzet, Denis. *La sagesse et le malheur: Michel de l'Hospital, Chancelier de France*. Seyssel, FR: Éditions Champ Vallon, 1998.

D'Aas, Bernard Berdou. *Jeanne III d'Albret: Chronique (1528–1572)*. Anglet, FR: Éditions Atlantica, 2002.

Daireaux, Luc. "Louis XIV et les protestants normands: autour de la révocation de l'édit de Nantes." *Bulletin de la Société de l'Histoire du Protestantisme Français* 158 (Jan.–Mar. 2012) 123–32. https://www.jstor.org/stable/24310203.

———. *Réduire les Huguenots: Protestants et pouvoirs en Normandie au XVIIe siècle*. Paris: Honoré Champion, 2010.

Daussy, Hugues. "Les huguenots entre l'obéissance au roi et l'obéissance à Dieu." *Nouvelle Revue du Seizième Siècle* 22.1 (2004) 49–69. https://www.jstor.org/stable/25599002.

———. *Les huguenots et le roi: Le combat politique de Philippe Duplessis-Mornay (1572–1600)*. Geneva: Droz, 2002.

Dentan, Yves. "Pierre Laporte, dit Rolland: Allocution." *Bulletin de la Société de l'Histoire du Protestantisme Français* 127 (Jan.–Mar. 1981) 185–90. https://www.jstor.org/stable/24295304.

De Waele, Michel. "Le cadavre du conspirateur: Peur, colère et défense de la communauté à l'époque de la Saint-Barthélemy." *Revue d'histoire moderne et contemporaine* 64.1 (Jan.–Mar. 2017) 97–115. http://www.jstor.org/stable/44986654.

Drévillon, Hervé, et al., eds. *Les dernières guerres de Louis XIV*. Rennes: Presses universitaires de Rennes, 2017. https://doi.org/10.4000/books.pur.155352.

Dreyss, Charles. *Mémoires de Louis XIV pour l'instruction du Dauphin*. Paris: Didier Libraires-Éditeurs, 1860. https://tinyurl.com/memoiresLouisXIV.

Dubled, Henri. "Les protestants français et l'étranger dans le Midi de 1685 à 1710: pour répondre à une vieille accusation." *Annales du Midi* 191 (1990) 427–49. https://doi.org/10.3406/anami.1990.3267.

Ducasse, André. *La guerre des Camisards: La résistance huguenote sous Louis XIV*. Paris: Librairie Hachette, 1978.

Dussaut, Charles. *Claude Brousson: Sa Vie, Son Ministère*. Toulouse: Imprimerie Chauvin, 1868.

BIBLIOGRAPHY

Encrevé, André. "Les huguenots du XIXe siècle." *Bulletin de la Société de l'Histoire du Protestantisme Français* 142 (Oct.–Dec. 1996) 547–85. https://www.jstor.org/stable/43498889.

———. *Les protestants et la vie politique française: De la Révolution à nos jours.* Paris: CNRS Éditions, 2020.

Engammare, Max. "Calvin monarchomaque? Du soupçon à l'argument." *Archiv für Reformationsgeschichte* 89 (1998) 207–26. https://doi.org/10.14315/arg-1998-jg14.

Félice, Guillaume de. *Histoire des Protestants de France: 1521–1787.* Vols. 1–4. 1880. Reprint. Marseille: Éditions Théotex, 2020.

Fléchier, Esprit. *Fanatiques et insurgés du Vivarais et des Cévennes.* Edited by Daniel Vidal. Grenoble: Jérôme Million, 1996.

———. *Lettres choisies de M. Fléchier.* Paris: Jacques Estienne, 1715. https://tinyurl.com/FlechierLettres.

———. *Œuvres complètes de Fléchier.* Vol. 5. Paris: Boiste Fils Ainé, 1827. https://tinyurl.com/FlechierOeuvres.

Fuller, Andrew Gunton. *The Complete Works of Rev. Andrew Fuller.* Philadelphia: American Baptist Publication Society, 1845.

Gachon, Paul. "L'œuvre de combat de Bâville en Languedoc." *Bulletin de la Société de l'Histoire du Protestantisme Français* 63.1 (Jan.–Feb. 1914) 51–67. https://www.jstor.org/stable/24290818.

Galand-Willemen, Perrine, and Loris Petris. *Michel de L'Hospital: Chancelier-Poète.* Geneva: Librairie Droz, 2020.

Garrisson, Janine, ed. *Histoire des Protestants en France: De la Réforme à la Révolution.* 2nd ed. Toulouse: Éditions Privat, 2001.

Joutard, Philippe. "Antoine Court et le désert: la force de l'histoire." *Bulletin de la Société de l'Histoire du Protestantisme Français* 157 (Jan.–Mar. 2011) 75–81. https://www.jstor.org/stable/24309921.

———. *Les Camisards.* Paris: Éditions Gallimard, 1976.

———. *La légende des Camisards: Une sensibilité au passé.* Paris: Éditions Gallimard, 1977.

Jurieu, Pierre. *Lettres Pastorales Addressées aux Fidèles de France Qui Gemissent Sous la Captivité de Babylon.* Rotterdam: Chez Abraham Acher, 1688. https://gallica.bnf.fr/ark:/12148/bpt6k3192456.

Lamothe, Alexandre de. *Les Camisards.* Paris: Librairie Blériot, 1898. https://tinyurl.com/LesCamisards.

Lemoine, Jean, ed. *Mémoires des évêques de France sur la conduite à tenir à l'égard des Reformés (1698).* Paris: Alphonse Picard, 1902. https://gallica.bnf.fr/ark:/12148/bpt6k33160f.

L'Ouvreleul, Jean-Baptiste. *Histoire du fanatisme renouvelé.* Edited by Patrick Cabanel. Montpellier: Presses du Languedoc, 2001.

Luria, Keith P. "Separated by Death? Burials, Cemeteries, and Confessional Boundaries in Seventeenth-Century France." *French Historical Studies* 24.2 (Apr. 2001) 185–222. https://doi.org/10.1215/00161071-24-2-185.

Lynn, John A. *Les guerres de Louis XIV.* Paris: Perrin, 2014.

BIBLIOGRAPHY

Maury, Léon. *Le réveil religieux dans l'Église reformée à Genève et en France: Étude historique et dogmatique (1810–1850)*. Paris: Librairie Fischbacher, 1892. https://archive.org/details/lerveilreligieuoomaurgoog.

Mazel, Abraham, et al. *Mémoires sur la guerre des Camisards*. Edited by Charles Bost. Montpellier: Presses du Languedoc, 2001.

Miquel, Pierre. *Les guerres de religion*. Paris: Fayard, 1980.

Misson, Maximilien. *Le théâtre sacré des Cévennes*. Montpellier: Presses du Languedoc, 1996.

Monahan, Gregory W. "Between Two Thieves: The Protestant Nobility and the War of the Camisards." *French Historical Studies* 30.4 (Oct. 2007) 537–58. https://doi.org/10.1215/00161071-2007-007.

———. *Let God Arise: The War and Rebellion of the Camisards*. Oxford: Oxford University Press, 2014.

Petitfils, Jean-Christian. *L'assassinat d'Henri IV: Mystères d'un crime*. Paris: Perrin, 2009.

Petit Robert de la Langue Française, Le Nouveau. Paris: Le Robert, 2007.

Pezet, Maurice. *L'Épopée des Camisards: Languedoc, Vivarais, Cévennes*. Barbentane, FR: Éditions Équinoxe, 1995.

Pouilly, Louis-Jean Lévesque de. *Vie de Michel de L'Hôpital, Chancelier de France*. London: David Wilson, 1764. https://archive.org/details/viedemicheldeloolv.

Poujol, Jacques. "Jean Cavalier." *Bulletin de la Société de l'Histoire du Protestantisme Français* 128 (Jan.–Mar. 1982) 93–99. http://www.jstor.org/stable/24295333.

Puaux, Frank. "Le dépeuplement et l'incendie des hautes-Cévennes." *Bulletin de la Société de l'Histoire du Protestantisme Français* 64.3 (Sept.–Oct. 1915) 592–618. https://www.jstor.org/stable/24288482.

———. "Origines, causes et conséquences de la guerre des Camisards." *Revue Historique* 129 (1918) 209–43. http://www.jstor.org/stable/40942016.

Puaux, Noé Antoine François. *Vie De Jean Cavalier . . . Avec Douze Gravures*. Strasbourg: Imprimerie du Vieux Berger, 1868.

Robinson, Timothy, and Philip Loft. "Religious Persecution and the World Watch List 2024." House of Commons Library, Jan. 23, 2024. https://tinyurl.com/4wesebec.

Rosa, Susan. "'Il était possible aussi que cette conversion fût sincère': Turenne's Conversion in Context." *French Historical Studies* 18.3 (Spring 1994) 632–66. https://www.jstor.org/stable/286687.

Roswalde, Hernand. *Jean Cavalier, ou les Camisards et les Cadets de la Croix (1702–1704)*. Paris: E. His. Éditeur, 1831. https://gallica.bnf.fr/ark:/12148/bpt6k5784183r.

Ruff, Pierre-Jean. *Les Camisards: Un combat pour la liberté de conscience*. Fontès, FR: Éditions Théolib, 2015.

Stéphan, Raoul. *L'Épopée huguenote*. Paris: La Colombe, 1945.

BIBLIOGRAPHY

Villars, Claude Louis Hector de. *Mémoires du maréchal de Villars (II)*. Paris: Librairie Renouard, 1887. https://archive.org/details/villars-memoires-du-marechal-de-villars-v-2.

Voltaire. *Le Siècle de Louis XIV*. Paris: Firmin Didot Frères, 1844. https://tinyurl.com/SiecledeLouisXIV.

Weiss, N. "Précisions documentaires sur l'histoire des Camisards." *Bulletin de la Société de l'Histoire du Protestantisme Français* 58.3 (May–June 1909) 243–53. https://www.jstor.org/stable/24287467.

Index

Affair of the Placards, 9, 89
Aigaliers, Baron of, 68–69, 72
Albret, Henry, 8
Albret, Jeanne d', 8, 17–18
Ancien Régime, 85
Anduze, 51
Anjou, Duke of (Francis), 17, 93
Arnaud, Étienne, 79
Austria, 21, 40

Bas-Languedoc, 22, 27, 39, 41–42,
Battle of Almanza, 73, 92
Battle of Champdomergue, 51, 91
Battle of Devois-de-Martignar-
 gues, 66, 92
Battle of Saint-Denis, 16–17
Bâville, Nicolas de Lamoignon de,
 32, 33– 35, 37, 40, 42, 47, 51,
 53, 55, 58, 61, 64, 66, 68–70,
 74, 91
Béarn, 28
Berwick, Marshal, 44, 73–74, 92
Beza, Theodore, 10–11, 15, 22
Bonbonnoux, Jacques, 52, 72–74,
 77, 93
Bost, Charles, 3, 87
Bourbon, Antoine de, 11
Bourbon Dynasty, 8, 11–12, 14, 85
Bourbon, Henry de. *See* Henry IV
Bourbon, Louis de (prince of
 Condé), 12

Bourlie, Antoine de la, 58
Bouton, Jacques, 42
Bres, Françoise, 43
Briçonnet, Guillaume (bishop), 8
Broglie, Victor Maurice, 33, 44,
 47, 51–54,
 68, 91
Brousson, Claude, 26–27, 34, 36,
 38,
 40–41, 48, 90–91
Brueys, David-Augustin, 2

Cadets de la Croix, 55–56, 61,
 64–65, 70
Calvière, Gaspard de, 48
Calvinism/Calvinist, x, 7, 24, 84
Calvin, John, x, 7–11, 15, 84, 89
Camisards, ix–xiii, xv–xvii, 2–3, 5,
 23, 46, 49–57, 60–66, 69–73,
 75–77, 79–82, 86–88, 91
Camisards Blancs, 55
Canillac, Marquis de, 58
Carbonnier-Burkard, Marianne,
 xvi
Castanet, 51, 54, 62, 73, 91–92
Catherine de' Medici, 12, 14–17,
 90
Catholic Church, xi, xvi, 1–4, 8–
 9, 15, 18, 23, 27, 29, 38, 42,
 76–77, 79, 84–86

Index

Catholicism, xi, 8, 10–11, 17–18, 24–25, 28–30, 36, 48–49, 54, 57, 79, 84–85, 90
Catinat (Abdias Maurel), 51, 53, 58, 74, 92
Cavalier, Jean, xi, xvii, 44, 47–48, 50–51, 53–55, 58, 60, 63–67, 70–73, 75, 92–93
Cévennes, xi, xv, xvii, 2, 22–23, 27, 29, 31–34, 39, 41–42, 44–45, 47–48, 50–51, 55, 57–59, 67–68, 72–75, 79, 88, 91–92
Chabert, Pierre, 54
Chaila Abbot du (François de Langlade), 2–3, 32, 43, 45, 46–47, 91
Chamillart, Michel, 47, 52, 56, 69, 73, 75
Charles I (England), 24
Charles II (England), 24
Charles IX (France), 14, 16–17
Charles X (France), 85, 93
Church of England, 24
Church of the Desert, xvi, 38, 39–40, 77–81
Circle of Meaux, 8–9
Claris, Pierre, 44, 73–75,
Coligny, Admiral Gaspard de, 14–15, 17
Concordat (Rome 1801), 84–86, 93
Confession of Faith, 10, 18, 89
Conspiracy of Amboise, 11–12, 89
Couderc, Jacques, 45
Couderc, Salomon, 31, 45, 47, 50, 60, 73
Council of Trent, 15, 89
Counter-Reformation, 89
Court, Antoine, x, xvii, 5, 77, 78–81, 93

Dauphiné, 22, 27–28, 33–34, 36–37, 40–41, 63

Declaration of the Rights of Man, 83
divine right (*droit divin*), 19
Dragonnades, 26–28, 31, 40, 68, 90
Dreyfus Affair, 86
Durand, Marie, 80

Edict of Amboise, 16–17, 90
Edict of Beaulieu, 17, 90
Edict of Fontainebleau. *See* Revocation of the Edict of Nantes
Edict of Grace (Peace of Alès), 19, 85, 90
Edict of January, 15, 16, 90
Edict (Peace) of Longjumeau, 90
Edict of Nantes, x–xi, 3, 18–19, 20, 24, 27–28, 32, 75, 78, 85–86, 90–91
Edict (Peace) of Saint-Germain, 17, 90
Edict of Toleration, 82, 93
England, 4, 23, 24, 28, 30, 38, 40, 73, 79
Enlightenment, 16
Estates-General, 15

Farel, William, 8
Fléchier, Bishop, 1, 4, 35, 42, 56, 91
Florentins, 55, 60–61
Francis I, 8–9, 89
Francis II, 11
Frederick William (Elector of Brandenburg), 30
freedom of conscience, 52, 58, 60, 65, 70–71, 82–83, 86–87
freedom of worship, x, 16–18, 20, 27, 34, 39, 40, 72, 86
French Revolution, 82–83, 93

Geneva, 4, 30, 48, 74, 84
Gentilshommes, 35, 53, 57, 62
Germany, 30
Guise, Francis of, 11, 16–17
Guise, Henry of, 17–18,
Guise, House of, 11, 12, 14–16

104

Index

Henry II, 11–12, 89
Henry III, 12, 17–18, 90
Henry IV (Henry of Navarre), xi, 3, 8, 16–17, 18, 19–20, 90
Huguenots, ix, xi, xv–xvi, 4, 7, 10–12, 15–18, 23–26, 28–29, 31–34, 43, 52, 55, 62, 78, 90
Hundred Years' War, 61

Institutes of the Christian Religion, 9, 89

James II, 28, 38
James V, 11
Jesuits, 23, 25
Jouany, 51, 53–55, 60, 73
Jubilee, 85, 94
Julien, Brigadier (Apostate), 52–55, 57–60, 62, 65, 68–69
July Revolution, 85, 93
Jurieu, Pierre, 31–32, 36, 38
Justification by faith, 8

LaBorde, Captain, 63
La Jonquière, 66
Lalande, Marquis de, 66–67
Lamothe, Alexandre, 3–4
Languedoc, 21, 22, 23, 26–27, 29, 32–33, 39–42, 52, 66, 68–70, 75, 82
Laporte, Gédéon, 47, 50–51, 53, 91
Laporte, Pierre (Roland), xvi, 44, 51–52, 54–55, 58–60, 63–64, 67, 70–72, 92
La Rochelle, xi, 9, 19, 28, 79, 90
La Rose, 59, 74
Lausanne, 38, 81, 93
La Valette, 37, 59
Law of Separation of Church and State, 86, 94
Lefèvre, Jacques, 8, 89
L'Hospital, Michel de, 14–15, 89
Lord's Supper (Eucharist), 15, 34, 42–43, 78

Loudun, 24, 90
Louis XIII, 3, 19–20, 90
Louis XIV, xi, xv–xvii, 3, 5–6, 20–21, 23–25, 27–28, 32, 37, 40, 47, 68, 71, 76, 78, 80, 86, 90, 93
Louis XV, 79, 80, 93
Louis XVI, 82, 93
Louis XVIII, 85, 93
Louis-Napoleon Bonaparte III, 85, 93
Louis-Philippe d'Orléans, 85, 93
Louvois, François, 23, 25, 35
L'Ouvreleul, Jean-Baptiste, 3
Lutherans, 7, 15, 84
Luther, Martin, ix, 7, 89

Maintenon, Madame de, 25
Manoël, Jean, 34
Marcilly, Colonel, 54
Marguerite of Navarre, 8–9, 89
Marguerite of Valois, 16–17, 90
Marie *La Blondine*, 51, 64
Marion, Élie, 31, 42, 59–60, 74
Marot, Clément, 8, 22
Mary Stuart, 11
Mathieu, Marie (*la Grande*), 51, 64
Mazarin, Cardinal, 20, 24
Mazel, Abraham, xvi, 31, 44–45, 50, 53, 60, 73–75, 92–93
Meaux, 8–9, 16, 89
Montauban, xi
Montpellier, 28, 41, 49, 67, 74, 80, 92
Montrevel, Marshal de, 44, 54–55, 57–61, 63–68, 91–92

Napoleon Bonaparte, 83, 84–86, 93
Navarre, Henry of. *See* Henry IV
Nérac, 8, 89
Nîmes, xi, 1, 20, 27–28, 35, 38, 43, 48–49, 53, 55, 63–64, 67, 69–70, 72, 74, 79, 92

Index

Nouveaux Convertis (New Converts), 3–4, 29–30, 35, 48, 54, 56–57, 60–62, 64–65, 69, 71, 77

Oliver Cromwell, 24
Organic Articles, 84, 86, 93

Peace of Alès. *See* Edict of Grace
Père La Chaise, 25
Pius VII (pope), 84
Planque, Brigadier, 63–64, 68, 73
Poul, Captain, 51, 53, 91
Preachers (*Prédicants*), xv, xvii, 31, 34, 37, 40, 51, 72, 87, 91
Prophetism, xii, xvi, 33, 37, 41, 43, 73, 77, 91
Prophets/Prophetesses, x–xiii, xv–xvii, 2, 31, 33, 36–37, 42–43, 51, 53, 60, 65, 72–73, 75, 77, 80, 87, 92
Protestantism, ix–xi, 9, 18, 22, 23, 25, 29, 34, 36, 38, 79–80, 87

Ravanel, 51, 53, 73–74, 92
Reformation, ix, xii, 1, 5, 7–8, 14, 22, 84
Reformed Church(es), xvii, 5, 10, 23, 37, 39, 77–78, 80, 84, 89
Religion Prétendue Réformée (RPR), See So-Called Reformed Religion
Renaissance, 8
Revocation of the Edict of Nantes, x, xv–xvii, 2–4, 21, 28–30, 32, 38, 48, 77, 79–80, 84–85, 91, 93
Rey, Fulcran, 34
Richelieu, Cardinal, 20, 85, 90
Roland. *See* Laporte, Pierre
Rome, 5, 9, 45, 84, 93
Roquelaure, Duke of, 75
Roquette, François, 80
Roux, Daniel, 41, 48

Saint-André, Marshal, 16

Saint Bartholomew's Day massacre, 17, 36n, 90
Schomberg, Duke of, 40
Séguier, Pierre (Esprit), 45–47, 91
Sixtus V (pope), 18
So-Called Reformed Religion, 18–19, 29, 76
Switzerland, 4, 27, 38–39, 58, 73
Synods, 10, 23–24, 78, 80, 85, 89–90, 93–94

Third Republic, 85, 94
Tower of Constance, 35, 48, 51–52, 74, 80, 92–93
Treaty of Ryswick, 40, 91
Turenne, Henry de la Tour d'Auvergne, 25

Valois Dynasty, 12
Vassy, Massacre of, 16, 90
Vatican, 86
Versailles, 28, 58, 66, 71–72
Vidal, Isaac, 34
Vilas De, 53
Villars, Marshal de, xvii, 44, 68–73, 92
Vincent, Isabeau, 36, 91
Vivarais, 27, 33–34, 37, 41, 65, 77, 91
Vivent, François, xvii, 34, 38–40, 91
Voltaire, xiii, xv, 20, 27, 47

Waldensians, 9
War of the Camisards (1702–1704), x–xii, xvi–xvii, 2, 5, 7, 13, 21, 32, 36, 44, 52, 76, 80–81, 86–88, 91
War of the Grand Alliance (1689–1697), 21
Wars of Religion (1562–1598), ix, xi, 1, 12, 14–16, 18, 90
War of Spanish Succession (1701–1714), 21
William III (of Orange), 38

www.ingramcontent.com/pod-product-compliance
Lightning Source LLC
Chambersburg PA
CBHW071219160426
43196CB00012B/2351